FUTURES OF BLACK POWER

FRONTIERS OF THE AMERICAN SOUTH

UNIVERSITY PRESS OF FLORIDA

Florida A&M University, Tallahassee
Florida Atlantic University, Boca Raton
Florida Gulf Coast University, Ft. Myers
Florida International University, Miami
Florida State University, Tallahassee
New College of Florida, Sarasota
University of Central Florida, Orlando
University of Florida, Gainesville
University of North Florida, Jacksonville
University of South Florida, Tampa
University of West Florida, Pensacola

Futures of Black Power
Reimagining the Black Past

Edited by
Anthony M. Donaldson Jr.
and Madison W. Cates

Foreword by
William A. Link

UNIVERSITY PRESS OF FLORIDA
Gainesville/Tallahassee/Tampa/Boca Raton
Pensacola/Orlando/Miami/Jacksonville/Ft. Myers/Sarasota

Publication of this work made possible by a Sustaining the Humanities through the American Rescue Plan grant from the National Endowment for the Humanities.

Copyright 2025 by Anthony M. Donaldson Jr. and Madison W. Cates
All rights reserved
Published in the United States of America

30 29 28 27 26 25   6 5 4 3 2 1

Library of Congress Cataloging-in-Publication Data
Names: Donaldson, Anthony M., Jr, editor. | Cates, Madison W., editor. | Link, William A., author of foreword.
Title: Futures of black power : reimagining the black past / edited by Anthony M. Donaldson Jr. and Madison W. Cates ; foreword by William A. Link.
Description: 1. | Gainesville : University Press of Florida, 2025. | Series: Frontiers of the american south | Includes bibliographical references and index.
Identifiers: LCCN 2024025386 (print) | LCCN 2024025387 (ebook) | ISBN 9780813079295 (hardback) | ISBN 9780813080932 (paperback) | ISBN 9780813070971 (pdf) | ISBN 9780813073675 (ebook)
Subjects: LCSH: Black power—United States. | African Americans—Civil rights—United States. | African Americans—History—1964- | BISAC: HISTORY / African American & Black | HISTORY / United States / 20th Century
Classification: LCC E185.615 .F879 2025 (print) | LCC E185.615 (ebook) | DDC 323.1196/07309—dc23/eng/20241114
LC record available at https://lccn.loc.gov/2024025386
LC ebook record available at https://lccn.loc.gov/2024025387

The University Press of Florida is the scholarly publishing agency for the State University System of Florida, comprising Florida A&M University, Florida Atlantic University, Florida Gulf Coast University, Florida International University, Florida State University, New College of Florida, University of Central Florida, University of Florida, University of North Florida, University of South Florida, and University of West Florida.

University Press of Florida
2046 NE Waldo Road
Suite 2100
Gainesville, FL 32609
http://upress.ufl.edu

CONTENTS

Foreword   vii

Introduction   1
  Anthony M. Donaldson Jr. and Madison W. Cates

1. From "Freedom Now!" to "Black Power": An Oral History Interview with Kathleen Cleaver   16
2. Reflections on the Black Power Archive   25
   Ashley D. Farmer
3. "This Is Exactly What's Needed": An Oral History Interview with Dr. Gwendolyn Zoharah Simmons   42
4. The Case for a Black Power Oral History Digital Archive   53
   Jasmin A. Young
5. "Everybody's Born for Something": An Oral History Interview with Mabel Williams   71
6. "Mr. Muhammad Says All of This Is Possible for You and Me": Elijah Muhammad, *Muhammad Speaks,* and Black Nationalism during the Space Age   79
   D'Weston Haywood
7. Excerpt of Elijah Muhammad's Address from *Muhammad Speaks* (1962)   97
8. "Strength in Your Own Voice": An Oral History Interview with Nikki Giovanni   101

List of Contributors   107
Index   109

FOREWORD

Futures of Black Power: Reimagining the Black Past, edited by Anthony M. Donaldson Jr. and Madison W. Cates, is the fourth volume appearing in the University Press of Florida's Frontiers of the American South series. Our purpose in this series is to explore topics that push our understanding of what makes (and has made) the American South. Further, the series asks historians to consider different thematic approaches as well as new views about the historical meaning of the South, how it evolved, and the relevance of this evolution for our own time.

In this volume, the editors of *Futures of Black Power* add to the continuing expansions of both African American history and Black Power Studies by reimaging Black resistance and armed struggle. Into this nexus, the term "Black Power" originates. The term first appeared in Black novelist Richard Wright's nonfiction book *Black Power* (1954) but became best known after SNCC leader Stokely Carmichael famously used the phrase in a speech in October 1966. Donaldson and Cates explain how subsequent activists used Black Power to define their status apart from the classic Civil Rights Movement. That status grew out of Martin Luther King Jr.'s dependence on nonviolence, but it adopted a new mantra: Black freedom from racial oppression and white supremacy depended on the ability of Black men and women to defend themselves against police violence perpetrated against them.

Black Power has become a critical part of the ongoing debate among scholars: To what extent does southern history include African Americans? Like much of the scholarship about the history of the American South, research about Black Power reflects the centrality of race. African American history since the 1960s transformed the study of southern history. The arrival of forced migrants to the Western Hemisphere and of the first enslaved Africans subsequently led to the institutionalization of slavery; its incorporation into global capitalism; the painful emancipation of freed people by Civil War violence, and the establishment of Jim Crow de jure segregation.

Much of our misunderstanding of Black Power reflects a larger problem in sources that prevail in any scholarship about African Americans and reflects some of the work among southern historians. *Futures of Black Power* reconsiders Black Power by using a novel methodology and interpretive structure that blends the views of historians with first-person oral histories. Students of modern America, the Black experience, and the Civil Rights Movement will find much value in this collection.

William A. Link
Series Editor

Introduction

Anthony M. Donaldson Jr. and Madison W. Cates

From its inception, the Black Power Movement (BPM) not only advanced Black rights but also challenged the philosophical and intellectual framework of the Black Freedom Movement. Black Power produced Malcolm X's conception that freedom should occur "by any means necessary." The BPM started in June 1966 when Stokely Carmichael—a prominent leader with the Student Non-Violent Coordinating Committee (SNCC)—replaced the Civil Rights Movement's (CRM) notable call and response chant of "Freedom Now" with a bold-new rhetoric called "Black Power." The term "black power" (lowercase) was not new. The Black Power Movement (upper case) was different because it evolved beyond a phrase or rhetoric. At that particular moment, Black Power was defined by a group of people disillusioned by non-violence and status quo methods of organizing.

The BPM experienced immediate success. For instance, in October 1966, just four months after Carmichael's Black Power proclamation, Raymond Johnson, Huey P. Newton, and Robert "Bobby" Seale founded the Black Panther Party (BPP). Its emphasis on self-defense countered Martin Luther King Jr.'s more pacifist rhetoric. Looking back, BPP's militant persona shaped our early understanding of what we think of as Black Power. In addition to self-defense, however, BPP's ten-point program addressed Black disease with health clinics and poverty with free breakfast programs. The BPP embodied the ephemeral vision of the BPM. Overall, the movement instilled self-pride and self-reliance in Black people to loosen the physical and psychological grip of white supremacy. According to SNCC chairman Julian Bond, Black Power's influence and SNCC organizing destroyed "the psychological shackles which had kept black southerners in physical and mental peonage."[1]

What follows is an extension of what Peniel Joseph calls "Black Power Studies" from a futuristic perspective, taking the term "futuristic" literally, figuratively, and in other imaginative ways. The Black Power Studies subfield is still relatively new as defined by Joseph in 2009.[2] At the same time, Black Power archives—as demonstrated in this book's essays—have been subsumed by a plethora of CRM collections. How do we delineate between CRM and BPM archival material? In many instances, the Black Power subjects and sources are conflated with Civil Rights activists and materials. These blurred lines make it difficult to preserve the textual and oral histories of the BPM, thus undermining its unique place in the African American canon. This project aims to examine how we gather, preserve, and teach about Black Power for future generations of scholars, archivists, and students. In addition to framing the historical canon of Black Power Studies, *Futures of Black Power* considers Josh Myers's concept "Of Black Study," which delves into the lived experiences of Black individuals, alongside more conventional understandings of African American Studies programs that focus on Black courses, curricula, and the hiring of Black faculty. In essence, Black Study encompasses the lived realities of Black individuals outside of academia, long before predominantly white institutions formalized African American disciplines in the 1960s.[3] Similarly, the future of Black Power must reconcile traditional archiving, community organizing, and both visible and invisible references to capture the stories of its subjects.

Thus, there is a specific need to record and disseminate Black Power's primary sources, especially oral histories of movement activists as many continue to pass and others are getting older. Time is urgent. Of the original members of the BPP, only one remains living (Bobby Seale). One of the last living Black women from that era, Kathleen Cleaver, is nearly 80 years of age. In recognition of this urgency, we used Cleaver's oral history to set the stage for this project. Recording, collecting, and disseminating aging sources allows us to use firsthand accounts and meet subjects on their own terms. In many instances, former Black Power activists evolved from militant positions not because they abandoned who they were or what they stood for but rather for the opposite reasons. Black Power veterans lived long enough to witness the world change.

At some point, we must examine how Black Power evolved beyond the 1970s and the decline of the BPP. To do this, we must not only look at how the movement as a whole aged or expired but also track the trajectory of its parts—its living veterans. Doing this will allow us to find ways to associate age with space (i.e., like the Space Age), a movement without borders and formal order. Going forward, scholars must grapple with ageism within the field. In addition to much-needed research on topics such as queer sexualities and disability within Black Power Studies, we must interrogate the theories and treatment of its aging members. It may help to consider ways to incorporate ageism with Afrofuturism. How might we incorporate time and age into our understanding of the futures of Black Power? Our sources illustrating mid-twentieth-century Afrofuturism may help Black culture educators imagine using artistic works like George Clinton and the Parliament-Funkadelic, Sun Ra's *Space is the Place,* Outkast's *ATLiens,* and films like Marvel's *Black Panther* series as it pertains to Black utopias like Wakanda. Academicians, public historians, archivists, digital humanists, and graduate students will find value in the meta-discussions around our visions of Black Power Studies' future.

Looking ahead, Black Power Studies distinguishes itself from traditional Western archival methods by prioritizing what Ashley Farmer calls "disorderly" archives over institutional ones.[4] However, the dearth of Black Power archives creates challenges for Black Power Studies, especially for Historically Black Colleges and Universities (HBCUs) that lack resources. For instance, Black Power proponent and Congress of Racial Equality (CORE) director Floyd McKissick donated his papers to his alma mater North Carolina Central University—an HBCU—at the time of his death in 1991. However, today, his papers are listed and stored at the Southern Historical Collection (SHC) at the University of North Carolina at Chapel Hill. In late 2023, Wilson Library where the SHC is located, announced it would close for renovation for at least two years. Although UNC has since announced that Wilson Library will remain open in the short term, the threat of an extended closure is still looming.[5] Therefore a crucial piece of Black Power history would discontinue.

Also, permanent Black Power museums are non-existent. As a result, archival materials related to the BPM often end up displaced or inaccessible. This lack of permanent housing for documents contributes to misunderstandings of Black Power both as a field of study and as a practice. In reimagining power through the perspectives and identities of Black Power activists, readers are compelled to confront the revolutionary nature of their stories. Ultimately, the absence of traditional artifacts and permanent housing for documents underscores the need to engage with Black Power on its own terms, outside the confines of white institutions.

But as much as BPM instilled racial pride, it was the simultaneously practical and imaginative solutions offered by its groups and individuals that attracted millions of Blacks into its rank and file. The public display of racial pride such as "afro" hairstyles, "hip" speeches, and African dashiki clothing was a necessary step to reverse Black mental bondage that in some ways assimilated to white customs by straightening their hair, "talking white," and wearing Eurocentric dress. In short, BPM—by looking backward through the lens of an African people—created yet another pathway for Black people to imagine a better future. Black media also aided this process. The Nation of Islam (NOI) had long since established Black-owned enterprises and media with *The Final Call* and *Muhammed Speaks,* but other Black outlets like *Ebony* and *Jet* magazine rolled out unapologetic images of Black people draped in Afrocentric dashikis and afro hairstyles. Moreover, as historian D'Weston Haywood argues in his book *Let Us Make Men,* "influential Black newspapers used the rhetoric and strategy of redeeming Black manhood to propel the Black freedom struggle across the twentieth century."[6] These national images were compounded by James Brown's 1969 hit song that encouraged Blacks to "Say It Loud, I'm Black, and I'm Proud." At the same time, the BPM recaptured the image of Black identities and its leaders. *Ebony's* columnist and notable Black historian Lerone Bennett Jr. crowned Stokely Carmichael the "Architect of Black Power." This was a pivot away from white-owned media like the *Washington Post* which labeled Carmichael and others like him a menace or journalists such as Mike Wallace who portrayed the NOI and Malcolm X as "The Hate that Hate Produced."[7] Reclaiming images of Black Power's past helps set new standards going forward.

At the same time, the BPM connected Black America's plight to an international struggle against imperialism. Stretching back into the mid-nineteenth century, historian Paul Ortiz argues that emancipation was liberation and revolution was a global phenomenon fought for by workers under imperial rule.[8] BPP carried this outlook. In their work, *Black Against Empire,* Josh Bloom and Waldo Martin reveal how Black Americans saw their lives in the inner cities as analogous to those under colonial rule, exploited by capitalism and controlled by the police. As CORE director Floyd McKissick observed, Black Americans were part of a struggle of all the "downtrodden to get rid of racism, capitalism, and imperialism." At that same time, antipoverty worker Howard Fuller organized an African Liberation Day that raised thousands of dollars and supplied resources for colonized countries.[9] McKissick was also engaged with the most funded Black capitalist project in American history when an unlikely ally in President Richard Nixon approved over 20 million dollars to build his Black utopia of Soul City. The future of Black Power will also have to grapple with these seemingly contradictive dilemmas faced by its subjects. Anthony M. Donaldson Jr.'s article published in 2023 referred to these seemingly opposing forces within the BPM as a "Black Power paradox."[10] BPM's impact and paradoxes echo far and resound to this day.

But as much as the BPM's bravado promoted pride, its violent reputation led to the death of key figures and the movement itself. Racial uprisings included, but were not limited to, Watts (1965), Newark (1967), and Detroit (1968). The most costly occurred in Miami in 1980. The Revolutionary Action Movement (RAM), Black Liberation Army, and MOVE transitioned from BPP's self-defense tactics to guerrilla warfare. Although most Black Power activists were not violent, the perception of universal violence led to the creation of FBI programs such as COINTELPRO that persecuted violent and nonviolent Black leaders alike. The meteoric rise and fall of the BPM created more questions than it resolved. Although BPM organized the Black ghettoes, it was incomplete and wrought with jail and death. As a result, for many, Black Power became synonymous with anti-American violence and urban uprisings, as these dynamic strands of the movement contained revolutionary potential that disrupted American history.

Subsequently, these bold ideas and organizations changed the landscape of Black scholarship. As Carmichael and Hamilton wrote in their 1967 book *Black Power*, the movement intended to "ask the right questions, to encourage a new consciousness and to suggest new forms which express it."[11] Such ideas not only shaped Black politics but also the direction of Black Studies in the academy. For example, in the first essay of this volume, Ashley Farmer charts this contested discourse. She argues that recent scholarship about Black Power establishes the topic as a "viable branch of American and African American history."[12]

Chronologically and thematically, the year 1966 marked not simply the rise of BPM or the demise of CRM but rather a turning point for new ways of thinking and achieving Black freedom. Part of the misinterpretation of our Black Past is rooted in the false binaries between BPM and CRM that contrast strategies of violence from non-violence or separatism from integrationism. But these binaries are oversimplifications. In 1960 Ella Baker, famed Civil Rights organizer and Executive Director of the Southern Christian Leadership Conference (SCLC), noted: "The Student Leadership Conference [in Raleigh] made it crystal clear that current sit-ins and other demonstrations are concerned with something much bigger than a hamburger or even a giant-sized Coke."[13] In 1966, Carmichael echoed Baker's sentiments to a majority-white crowd at the University of

California at Berkeley as he claimed the "question is not one of integration or segregation. Integration is a man's ability to want to move in there by himself." In this instance, CRM and BPM shared a common goal of Black freedom. However, the BPM expanded and advanced the possible means to achieve that goal.[14]

Historian Wesley Hogan reminds us that, although SNCC's identity early on was built through a culture of common struggle, the lack of a unified vision and multiple issues regarding philosophical differences caused it to crumble. These internal fissures within SNCC and the Black Freedom Movement more broadly created a vacuum for new ideas.[15] Subsequently, Black Power not only entered into the political discourse of the times but also joined the intellectual framework of history.

As historian David Blight explains, the Civil War as a "regenerative-conception . . . launched Black freedom and future equality" on a "marvelous" yet "endangered" course in American history and memory. What many call America's Second Reconstruction, the CRM birthed new promises for Black people that were unmet by America's first Reconstruction.[16] In relationship to Blight, one of the leading Black Power Studies scholars—as well as a participant in the early conversations that formed the basis of this book—historian Hasan Kwame Jeffries's *Bloody Lowndes* reminds us that "freedom rights" began immediately after the Civil War and extended beyond the traditional chronology of the CRM.[17] In this instance, the struggle for black power (in the lowercase sense) was always present in American history but less visible in America's memory. The erasure of "freedom rights" caused partly by white supremacy, mob violence, and Jim Crow was exacerbated by revisionist histories led by the William Dunning School, a school of thought that victimized the Confederate States of America. The political and historical ramifications were dire. What remained from Dunning were scattered and fragmented parts of the Black past.[18]

Robin D. G. Kelley's *Freedom Dreams: The Black Radical Imagination* looks at the long legacy of freedom struggles and its various forms. Originally, Kelley grappled with the question of what happened to all the radical movements from the 1960s that promised change. To help reconcile these questions in Black history, Kelley suggests Black activists from the sixties "looked back" at emancipation "in search of a better future."[19] During his "I Have a Dream" speech, Dr. Martin Luther King Jr. surmised, "America had defaulted on [its] promissory note insofar as her citizens of color were concerned." In short, we look to reexamine and reimagine a Black past to create a better future for Black Power Studies.[20]

When Kimberly Drew and Jenna Wortham published their edited collection, *Black Futures* in early 2020, the authors explored one pivotal question: "What does it mean to be Black and alive right now?" The urgency of this question subsequently only grew more complicated in the following months.[21] Already ravaged by the pandemic, the public response to George Floyd and Breonna Taylor's murders spurred national attention. Subsequently, politicians, universities, and even banks vowed to confront racial injustices, at least in theory.[22] As much as class impacts Black life, Black Power's gender and sexual politics persist. In 2015, the "Say Her Name" campaign, in the aftermath of Sandra Bland's death, crossed gender, racial, sexual, and global lines. "Say Her Name" was a deliberate effort to recognize Black victims as real people and to further prove that Black Lives Matter. But as much as we gasped at the visible brutality of Sandra Bland on camera it was the invisible violence that cost her life that haunted Black America. Her death, like so many others before, was left to our imagination. Once again, the horrific Black experience took place off stage—behind the veil of state-sponsored incarceration—undocumented off camera. These intersectional patterns trend to Black Power's contemporary relevance.

This volume, seeking to explore these questions and contribute to the scholarly conversation, is an outgrowth of scholarly conversations begun in 2020. We intend to expand on Joseph's suggestion of the new field of "Black Power Studies" in the complexity of the digital, archival, and imaginative dimensions of Black Power.[23] We explore and reimagine the state of the Black Power documentary past in essays by Ashley Farmer and Jasmin Young as well as examine key institutions and figures in Black history in D'Weston Haywood's essay. Interspersed within these scholarly pieces are excerpts from oral histories with Kathleen Cleaver, Gwendolyn Zoharah Simmons, and Mabel Williams. This collection concludes with two pieces—a speech from Elijah Muhammad and an interview with poet Nikki Giovanni—that flesh out the range of Black intellectual ferment and Afrofuturism. In providing space for Black activists, movement leaders, and thinkers to tell their stories, this collection seeks to further underscore the need for recording and archiving these histories.

In doing so, this approach seeks to apply to studies of the Black Freedom Struggle Barbara Fields's admonition to southern historians that "there are no tragic flaws or central themes in which to take shelter . . . There are only acts and decisions of men and women in a society now past."[24] Centering the experiences, voices, and memories of Black women and men is central to this specific project and the broader, urgent work of remembering the recent American past. Together, these essays and documents not only consider Black Power's role in the historical literature but also, we hope, will scrutinize the extent to which the movement's path shaped the future of the ongoing African American freedom struggle.

Futures of Black Power brings together three historians who study the history of the BPM. Although these papers differ in their approach or topical lens, they collectively provide a new perspective on a dynamic field by illustrating the diverse ways that African Americans tried to achieve change in the early 1960s. In offering new histories of Black Power, these essays exemplify the turn in recent scholars' approach to the movement's relationship with capitalism, gender, and intellectual forces.

Featuring a keynote essay by Ashley Farmer, this collection reconceptualizes the BPM's place in American memory. Jasmin Young and D'Weston Haywood take up Farmer's point about building Black Power archives by deftly deploying oral histories and print sources. In doing so, they collectively advance the idea that historians must reassert the centrality and continuity of Black Power politics to the grand arc of African American history. Together these historians help us traverse Black Power's dynamic growth in the Western canon.

This collection is not an attempt to validate or "sanction" Black Power. In 2017, McArthur Fellow and acclaimed Black artist Kerry James Marshall told National Public Radio (NPR) that a Black presence in the art world was "not negotiable." "There are fewer representations of black figures in the historical record," Marshall further maintained, and Black Power's presence in American history is "not negotiable."[25] This edited collection not only recontextualizes Black Power but also allows us to excavate the impact of Blackness in contributing to and challenging the Western canon both in imaginative and real ways. We recognize the radical tradition of Black intellectuals—including David Walker, Phillis Wheatley, Frederick Douglass, Harriet Jacobs, Martin Delaney, W.E.B. Du Bois, Booker T. Washington, James Weldon Johnson, Zora Neale Hurston, and Cedric Robinson—exists with and without outside approval. However, the formal exclusion of Black people from historical writing requires this rewriting and reexamination.

Although the BPM is rooted in actual subjects and events, our memories and interpretations of the past rely on a collection of sources and methodologies. How we interpret the BPM revolves around how one accesses and processes BPM information. Young's essay in this collection poignantly states "to date, there are over 1533 oral history collections dedicated to the

Civil Rights Movement." Yet despite breakthroughs in collecting and preserving a CRM past, "the Black Power Movement, however, has none."[26]

Black primary sources and archives are a common strand linking these futures of Black Power. Black sources empower Black subjects. Some of the earliest and most cited Black sources derive from the WPA Projects' Slave Narratives. Today digital collections such as SNCC's Digital Gateway possessed by Duke University offer a breakthrough for Civil Rights scholarship and legacy maintenance. The proliferation of these legacies was well organized and preserved. Black Power sources are more fragmented, hence the consensus on Black Power–related events and figures seems less cohesive.

In offering new histories of Black Power, these essays exemplify how existing currents in the field approach the movement's relationship with capitalism, gender, and intellectual thought, while also pointing the way forward to new avenues for research and public engagement. The collective, scholarly thrust of these essays points to the need for a deeper understanding of the ways that Black Power activists created and sustained the spaces of communal protest, care, and preservation. In different but related ways, the arguments of these essays emphasize the need for community institutions and spaces to preserve and promote Black history in all its myriad forms.

Using case studies from archival theory, memory studies, and ideological production, *Futures of Black Power* provides a unique perspective into the field's past, present, and potential paths ahead. Of course, historians should always be careful not to predict the future of academic study, political movements, or anything of the like. Instead, this collection aims to call attention to the dynamic field of Black Power Studies and suggest new paths for deeper intellectual and community engagement. These essays offer a snapshot in time, showing the field's ongoing reinvention with its rich variety and its yet untapped potential for new work. In doing so, there is something that current and future scholars can learn from how Black Power historians see their subjects, their craft, and the state of the field over a half-century removed from the BPM's emergence.

In the first essay of this collection, Ashley Farmer offers a compelling framework for developing Black Power archives. As she makes clear here, doing African American history requires different forms of intellectual production than in the past. Visiting established archives and relying on well-worn source material from subject files or institutional collections is often not enough. As Farmer sees it, the "disorderly distributed" nature of "the Black Power archive" is not necessarily a hindrance to the field's development.[27] Instead, it can be an asset, enhancing the dynamic and innovative methods of the field. Such versatility in collecting and interpreting source material, in Farmer's view, has helped and will continue to aid Black Power scholars to disrupt misleading narratives about the movement as male-dominated in leadership and geographically constrained to urban centers in the North, to name just two examples.

In doing so, Farmer's essay reconceptualizes the archive as a space for liberation. Other scholars of the BPM should see this as both a comfort and a challenge. Creating a "Black Power Archival Ethic," as Farmer suggests, could help to circumvent the surveilling and disciplining tendencies of government or other institutional archives. Through what she terms the "disorderly, disobedient, and oppositional collection of the Black Power archives," especially in an ever more digital age, historians can work for more accessible and collaborative spaces to work with activists, archivists, and communities.

Picking up on Farmer's call for scholars to support or develop Black Power archives, Jasmin Young's essay here addresses the dearth of oral history collections dedicated to the study of the BPM. As her starting point, Young contrasts the over 1500 oral history collections focused on studying the CRM with the total absence of oral history archives centering on the BPM.[28] Building on the work of scholars like Ashley Farmer, Rhonda Williams, and Robyn Spencer, her essay here and broader scholarship demonstrates the mutually beneficial relationship between oral histories and the gender politics of the BPM.[29]

Moreover, Young's work emphasizes how better collecting and categorizing interviews with Black Power activists can allow scholars to tap into "family histories of resistance." In doing so, rethinking methodological approaches can produce radically different research. Building digital and oral history archives like the kind envisioned here could not only change the way that research is done—namely making it more effective and efficient through better categorization and greater access—but it could reveal deeper and richer histories of Black community organizing. In support of this point, Young offers helpful examples from her own research. As a graduate student, her dogged pursuit in search of a deeper understanding of Mabel Williams's life as more than just "Robert F. Williams's widow" is recounted here as a cautionary tale and a source of inspiration for her project to create the Black Power Digital Archive (BPDA).[30]

D'Weston Haywood reminds us that through the Nation of Islam's newspapers, we learn that Elijah Muhammad not only wanted Black people to separate themselves from American society but perhaps settle on their own planet. Regardless of the practicality of Muhammad's message as interpreted by readers, Muhammad as a source of a radical Black imaginary teaches us that we must reconsider how we process and remember intellectual and imaginative expanses in organizational histories of resistance. According to Haywood, "Muhammad was among the first Afro-futurists, working to expand Black politics by articulating visions of Black liberation located in another space and time."[31] Equally important to this intellectual project was the Black sourcing and proliferation of Muhammad's Afrofuturist ideas. For instance, NOI's official news organ, *Muhammad Speaks*, gave vivid form to these radical ideas.

Since scholars have produced substantial studies in the last decade on the international dimensions of the Black Freedom Struggle and the Black Radical Tradition, Haywood's work here and elsewhere on the NOI helps to expand the spatial limits of those discussions. If anticolonialism offered a means of Black global liberation for the activists and intellectuals studied by Penny Von Eschen and others, Elijah Muhammad's radical, Afrofuturist vision of a Black planet was something both related and different.[32] Rather than fanciful thinking, in Haywood's rendering, Muhammad's ideas offer a means of "spiritual empowerment" as part of "an ever-changing racial and political imaginary."[33]

Between each of these essays are primary sources that build on the collective thrust of this work that more should be done to document and preserve the history of the BPM. The editors and contributors selected each "vignette" both to elucidate the themes explored in our analyses and to speak to the potential for a more concerted, thoughtful effort to preserve this history. Respective oral history interviews with Kathleen Cleaver, Gwendolyn Zoharah Simmons, Mabel Williams, and Nikki Giovanni are paired with an excerpt from Elijah Muhammad's *Muhammad Speaks* to better explicate the meaning of the BPM for generations past, present, and future.

The inclusion of these oral histories and primary sources helps illustrate what Black Power—its ideas, organizations, and trajectory—meant to those activists and leaders who were its beating heart. Over the last four decades, there have been robust scholarly conversations around the contested nature of civil rights memory.[34] As Mabel Williams discusses in her interview with historian David Cecelski, the BPM's legacy has not been celebrated with the kind of consensus-driven, often-misleading memorializations that prompted civil rights historians to critique America's collective memory of that movement. However, future historians should take up Farmer and Young's points about rethinking the archive and consider the role of what other scholars have termed "collected"—rather than collective—memory to underscore how individual memories can shape our common understanding of the past.[35] In that vein, the essays and primary sources contained here will hopefully serve to reinforce the message that more can be done to bring discussions about memory and the archive to the fore of Black Power Studies.

For Farmer, Black Power futures exist in the archives whereas Haywood's work excavates NOI's celestial Black nation-building, and Young's essay re-centers Black women in the digital archives. In each case, these authors grapple with Black Power futures by decolonizing archival spaces and rethinking "Black Power Studies" and their subjects. Black Power subjects were futuristic in their own right. By considering the future of Black Power then and now we escape the traditional ways of processing information and instead preserve a legacy as it was intended.

Notes

1 Julian Bond, "SNCC: What We Did," *Monthly Review,* 52: 5, October 1, 2000, https://monthlyreview.org/2000/10/01/sncc-what-we-did/ (accessed July 22, 2022).
2 Peniel Joseph, "The Black Power Movement: A State of the Field," *The Journal of American History* 96: 3 (December 2009): 751–776.
3 Joshua Myers, *Of Black Study* (London: Pluto Press, 2023).
4 See Chapter 2 of this collection and Ashley D. Farmer, "Disorderly Distribution: The Dispersal of Queen Mother Audley Moore's Archives and the Illegibility of Black Women Intellectuals," *The Black Scholar* 52: 4 (October 2022): 5–15.
5 "Acquisitions Information" in Floyd B. McKissick Papers #4930, Southern Historical Collection of the University of North Carolina at Chapel Hill and the African American Resources Collection of North Carolina Central University; Jessica Walker, "Wilson Library Construction Timeline Extended, Library Open to the Public for the Foreseeable Future," *The Daily Tar Heel,* March 3, 2024, https://www.dailytarheel.com/article/2024/03/university-wilson-library-construction-extended (accessed March 14, 2024).
6 D'Weston Haywood, *Let Us Make Men: The Twentieth-Century Black Press and a Manly Vision for Racial Advancement* (Chapel Hill: University of North Carolina Press, 2018), 234.
7 Lerone Bennett Jr., "Stokely Carmichael: Architect of Black Power," *Ebony* (September 1966), 26–27.
8 Paul Ortiz, "Washington, Toussaint, and Bolivar, 'The Glorious Advocates of

Liberty': Black Internationalism and Reimagining Emancipation," 187–215, in James J. Broomall and William A. Link, eds., *Rethinking American Emancipation: Legacies of Slavery and the Quest for Black Freedom* (Cambridge, UK: Cambridge University Press, 2016).

9   Joshua Bloom and Waldo E. Martin, *Black Against Empire: The History and Politics of the Black Panther Party* (Berkeley: University of California Press, 2016).
10 Anthony M. Donaldson Jr., "'So Why Can't They Finance Black Power?' Howard Lamar Fuller's Fight for Black Control of Housing in North Carolina, 1965–1969," *Essays in Economic & Business History* 41: 2 (November 2023): 186–207.
11 Kwame Ture (Stokely Carmichael) and Charles V. Hamilton, *Black Power: The Politics of Liberation in America* (New York: Vintage Books, 1967, 1992), 13.
12 Ashley Farmer, "Reflections on the Black Power Archive."
13 Ella Baker, "Bigger Than a Hamburger," *Southern Patriot* 18 (May/June 1960), in Manning Marable and Leith Mullings, eds. *Let Nobody Turn Us Around: Voices of Resistance, Reform and Renewal*, Second Edition (Oxford: Rowan & Littlefield Publishers, 2009), 393–394.
14 Stokely Carmichael, Speech at UC Berkeley, October 29, 1966, transcript via *Voices of Democracy: The U.S. Oratory Project,* University of Maryland, https://voicesofdemocracy.umd.edu/carmichael-black-power-speech-text/.
15 Wesley Hogan, *Many Minds, One Heart: SNCC's Vision for a New America* (Chapel Hill: University of North Carolina Press, 2007).
16 David Blight, *Race and Reunion: The Civil War in American Memory* (Cambridge, MA: Belknap Press of Harvard University Press, 2001), 18.
17 Hasan Kwame Jeffries, *Bloody Lowndes: Civil Rights and Black Power in Alabama's Black Belt* (New York: New York University Press, 2009), esp. 2–4.
18 The literature on Reconstruction is voluminous, but for our purposes here, the following works should be consulted: William Dunning, *Reconstruction: Economic and Political, 1865–1877,* (New York: Harper & Brothers, 1907); W.E.B Du Bois, *Black Reconstruction: An Essay Toward a History of the Part Which Black Folk Played in the Attempt to Reconstruct Democracy in America, 1860–1880* (New York: Atheneum, 1935, 1982); Kenneth M. Stampp, *The Era of Reconstruction 1865–1877: A Revisionist View of One of the Most Controversial Periods in American History,* (New York: Alfred A. Knopf, 1970); Eric Foner, *Reconstruction: America's Unfinished Revolution, 1863–1877* (New York: Harper & Row, 1988); Heather Cox Richardson, *West from Appomattox: The Reconstruction of America after the Civil War* (New Haven: Yale University Press, 2007); Steven Hahn, *A Nation Under Our Feet: Black Political Struggles in the Rural South from Slavery to the Great Migration* (Cambridge, MA: The Belknap Press of Harvard University Press, 2003).
19 Robin D.G. Kelley, *Freedom Dreams: The Radical Black Political Imagination* (New York: Basic Books, 2002), 15.
20 Dr. Martin Luther King Jr., "I Have a Dream," August 28, 1963, transcript via *National Public Radio,* January 18, 2010, https://www.npr.org/2010/01/18/122701268/i-have-a-dream-speech-in-its-entirety (accessed June 10, 2022).

21 Kimberly Drew and Jenna Wortham, eds., *Black Futures* (New York: Random House, 2020), xiii.
22 For instance, as of 2021, America's top public companies have committed $50 billion to combat racial inequality since Floyd's murder. A deeper look reveals that 90 percent of these funds—$45.2 billion—were loans that could profit companies. Tracy Jan, Jena McGregor, and Meghan Hoyer, "Corporate America's $50 Billion Promise," *Washington Post*, August 23, 2021, https://www.washingtonpost.com/business/interactive/2021/george-floyd-corporate-america-racial-justice/. (accessed June 8, 2022).
23 Peniel Joseph, "State of the Field," *The Journal of American History* 96: 3 (December 2009): 751–776; See also: Joseph, *Waiting 'Til the Midnight Hour: A Narrative History of Black Power* (New York: Henry Holt, 2006); Rhonda Williams, *Concrete Demands: The Search for Black Power in the 20th Century* (New York: Routledge, 2015), 4.
24 Barbara Anne Fields, "Ideology and Race in American History," in *Region, Race, and Reconstruction: Essays in Honor of C. Vann Woodward*, eds. J. Morgan Kousser and James M. McPherson, (New York: Oxford University Press, 1982), 169.
25 Kerry James Marshall, quoted in Susan Stamberg, "Kerry James Marshall: A Black Presence In The Art World Is 'Not Negotiable,'" *National Public Radio*, March 28, 2017, https://www.npr.org/2017/03/28/521683667/kerry-james-marshall-a-black-presence-in-the-art-world-is-not-negotiable.
26 Jasmin Young, "The Case for a Black Power Oral History Digital Archive."
27 Ashley Farmer, "Reflections on the Black Power Archive."
28 Jasmin Young, "The Case for a Black Power Oral History Digital Archive," page 3.
29 Rhonda Y. Williams, "Black Women and Black Power," *OAH Magazine of History* 22, no. 3 (2008): 22–26; *Concrete Demands: The Search for Black Power in the 20th Century* (New York: Routledge, 2015); Robyn C. Spencer, *The Revolution Has Come: Black Power, Gender, and the Black Panther Party in Oakland* (Durham: Duke University Press, 2016); Ashley D. Farmer, *Remaking Black Power: How Black Women Transformed an Era* (Chapel Hill: University of North Carolina Press, 2017).
30 Young, "The Case for a Black Power Oral History Digital Archive," page 15.
31 See, for example, Mark Dery, "Black to the Future: Interviews with Samuel R. Delany, Greg Tate, and Tricia Rose," in Mark Dery, *Flame Wars: the Discourse of CyberCulture*, (Durham: Duke University Press, 1994), 179–222; Francesca T. Royster, "Labelle: Funk, Feminism, and the Politics of Flight or Fight," *American Studies*, 52:4 (2013): 77–98; William Sites, *Sun Ra's Chicago: Afrofuturism and the City* (Chicago: University of Chicago Press, 2020).
32 Penny M. Von Eschen, *Race Against Empire: Black Americans and Anticolonialism, 1937–1957* (Ithaca: Cornell University Press, 1997); see also: Gerald Horne, *Black and Red: W.E.B. Du Bois and the Afro-American Response to the Cold War, 1944–1963* (Albany: SUNY Press, 1986); Horne, *Mau Mau in Harlem? The U.S. and the Liberation of Kenya* (New York: Palgrave Macmillan, 2009); Carol Anderson, *Bourgeois Radicals: The NAACP and the Struggle for Colonial Liberation, 1941–1960* (Cambridge: Cambridge University Press, 2014); Brenda Gayle Plummer, *In Search*

of Power, African Americans in the Era of Decolonization, 1956-1974 (Cambridge: Cambridge University Press, 2013).

33 D'Weston Haywood, "'Mr. Muhammad Says All of This is Possible for You and Me:' Elijah Muhammad, Muhammad Speaks, and Black Nationalism during the Space Age," 2022, Paper in Possession of Authors; Robin D. G. Kelley, *Race Rebels: Culture, Politics, and the Black Working Class,* (New York: Free Press, 1996), 42-43.

34 For example, see: Jacquelyn Dowd Hall, "The Long Civil Rights Movement and the Political Uses of the Past," *Journal of American History* 91: 4 (2005): 1233-1263; Steven Lawson, "Long Origins of the Short Civil Rights Movement," in *Freedom Rights: New Perspectives on the Civil Rights Movement,* edited by Danielle McGuire and John Dittmer (Lexington: University Press of Kentucky, 2011), 9-37; Renee C. Romano and Leigh Raiford, eds., *The Civil Rights Movement in American Memory* (Athens, GA: University of Georgia Press, 2006); Jeanne Theoharis, *A More Beautiful and Terrible History: the Uses and Misuses of Civil Rights History* (Boston: Beacon Press, 2018); and Scott A. Sandage, "A Marble House Divided: The Lincoln Memorial, the Civil Rights Movement, and the Politics of Memory, 1939-1963," *The Journal of American History* 80: 1 (June 1993): 135-167.

35 As historian W. Fitzhugh Brundage explains the concept, "this approach traces shared memories to individual experience and posits collective memory as the aggregation of such individual experience." W. Fitzhugh Brundage, "Southern History: Contentious and Collected," *Journal of Southern History* 75: 3 (August 2009): 751-766, quote on 754; Jeffrey K. Olick, "Collective Memory: The Two Cultures," *Sociological Theory* 17: 3 (November 1999): 333-348.

1

From "Freedom Now!" to "Black Power"

An Oral History Interview with Kathleen Cleaver

In this transcribed excerpt from a longer oral history interview, I (Donaldson) spoke with Kathleen Cleaver about her parents' involvement as community activists in the South. The full text of the interview is available through the Samuel Proctor Oral History Program archive. This interview was done during her visit to the University of Florida, while I was a graduate student there. Her family lived overseas for many years before she matriculated to Oberlin and Barnard for college. By 1966, she left college to take part in the Civil Rights Movement as an organizer of SNCC at the Atlanta, Georgia, headquarters. She eventually went to California and started organizing for the Black Panther Party and the Huey P. Newton campaign and talks about her experiences with the party. But to my surprise the BPP was a fledging organization. It was on the brink of collapse. Kathleen Cleaver along with her husband Eldridge Cleaver and a few teenagers gave it life. I sat for hours with Cleaver before and after the interview to discuss various topics that did not appear in the transcript. As much as she explores her experience during the Black Power Movement, so much is left off the record and left to the imagination. I can share that Kathleen Cleaver was clear the Black Lives Matter Movement differed from the Black Power Movement. Perhaps the future of Black power is rooted in the voices of its founding fathers and mothers like Kathleen Cleaver.

Anthony M. Donaldson Jr. [hereafter "D"]: I'm from Tennessee. I've read somewhere where you were organizing somewhere at Fisk at some point.

Kathleen Cleaver [hereafter "C"]: Fisk was a site where the Student Non-Violent Coordinating Committee held a conference. The conference was a Black student conference in the wake of the Black Power claim, the call for Black Power. How did we call it? We had a saying, "Liberation would come from a Black thing." That was a statement that I think

Jim Forman had made. That was a theme of a conference that we called in [19]67 to bring all the activist student groups to the Fisk campus, so we could all understand and learn about Black Power; the new phase.

D: Do you have a particular role or title—

C: I worked in a group called the "campus program." There were people who would travel to the campuses and organize students who were called campus travelers. My job was I basically stayed at the office and I wrote up documents, took notes at meetings, I typed stencils for a set of readings that we circulated so that there was a more comprehensive understanding of what Black Power was. I happen to have a copy that I found recently . . . I did office work, communications.

D: How did the conference go? Did it happen? Was there—

C: Well, it sort of happened in the sense that the facilities at Fisk University were available for a while. Anyways, the students came. The student activists that were plugged into SNCC managed to come to the campus because they had cars. There was a freak snowfall in the east coast that same weekend, so the adults that—writers, people like Leroy [LeRoi] Jones or Mary Baraka [Amiri Baraka], or Gwendolyn, not Gwendolen, Margaret Walker was in . . . Anyways, the writers and other adults never made it because—

D: You had these guys prepared to speak. They were coming to—

C: But they couldn't get there because of a blizzard. There were no flights. The only person who got to the conference who was scheduled to be a speaker was Eldridge Cleaver because he came from San Francisco. They ain't have any blizzards in San Francisco. [Laughter] We had all the SNCC activists and Eldridge Cleaver. That was our conference.

D: Had you known him at the time or was this your first time meeting—

C: Well, we had invited him to come to this conference. This was a SNCC conference and he is invited as a speaker and quite a few other people were invited as speakers, but he's the only one that managed to get there.

D: So this was your first time meeting him?

C: Many people's first time meeting him. [Laughter] Hadn't been out of prison very long. He had been out about three months.

D: From there, I'm just trying to coordinate the timeline, so you're working in SNCC—

C: In Atlanta.

D: In Atlanta. How do you end up going to California?

C: Well Eldridge Cleaver was from California and he was a prisoner and he was on parole. He got permission to come to our conference. To visit, the parole officer has to allow you to leave the jurisdiction. He came for a while. Then he had to go back to California. By the time he went back to California, he and I had gotten very interested in each other, so I wanted to see him again, I would have to go all the way to California because he wasn't allowed to leave again. They didn't like the fact that he come and hooked up with Stokely Carmichael and people like that. Stokely Carmichael was a big scary person back then.

D: Very scary.

C: He called for Black Power. It had never been done. And the time that he made the call, it was at night, and was in all the television shows because it was during something called the "Meredith March." There was a march across the Mississippi and at one night after he'd been arrested, they'd have these rallies and they would say, "What do we want? Freedom now, freedom now." After one night when he had been arrested and came back, stood up on the flatbed truck, and said, "No, no, no. Black Power. Black Power." So people started calling "Freedom Now" he figured the Civil Rights Act had handled the Freedom Now. His call for something other than [unclear] changed because Black Power is a political call. That's where the call was made in Mississippi on this Meredith March.

D: The "March against Fear."

C: Yes.

D: Okay. So, you ended up in California and—It just fascinates me how wherever you are, you are able to start organizing and getting—

C: No, we're in a movement. I'm not wherever I am. We're in a movement that's called the Civil Rights or Black Power Movement. They kind of merged because the Civil Rights Movement was what was attracting me, but by the time I got into it, Civil Rights had been passed, the Civil Rights Act. The movement became more of a—some people called it Black Liberation, some people called it Black Power, some people called it other things. But it was all Black. Whatever it was, it was—no Negro movement. It was Black movement. [Laughter].

D: Transitioning into I guess what becomes the Black Panther Party.

C: There was no Black Panther Party; not at the beginning.

D: Well, not yet.

C: Let's see. The Black Panther Party started in October of 1966. The Black Power call in Mississippi came . . .

D: June 1966.

C: Yeah. So, it was inspired. The Black Panther Party was inspired by the call for Black Power. The Black Panther Party didn't exist when the call came out.

D: Okay. It's the Black Panther Party of Self-Defense, but there's also other organizations that are splintering out—I think I read something—

C: There were several organizations that took that name. The Lowndes County Freedom Organization which was a political party that was created to implement the call for Black power in Lowndes County which was a 80 percent Black county that no one had every voted in. They used that project—SNCC used that project as a demonstration of Black power. The word is out there; the concept is out there. There were Black Power groups, people with different kinds of names implying that they are supporting Black Power, Black consciousness groups, Black cultural groups. It became a very, very exciting new way of organizing and people sort of throwing off this notion because [the] concept of Negro became associated with segregation. Not that it has to be, but that's because that's what we were rejecting. So Black is associated with liberation and independence, end of colonialism, end of segregation. That's how it was interpreted. So Black was something brand new, consciousness-wise.

D: Okay. I wasn't saying that everywhere you went it was going on. It was just—

C: I went to places where stuff was already going on.

D: I see, I see. You knew where to be.

C: Well, I came to Atlanta and joined SNCC. I was living in New York, but the people I knew in New York, their organization was based in Atlanta. So I came down to Atlanta, worked in the headquarters of the Student Non-Violent Coordinating Committee which was in the process of basically disintegrating. It had been a very huge operation with a big budget and a big building. By the time SNCC was identified with Black Power, it kind of cratered and a lot of the money left and people left. It had a big office, but very small staff and no income.

D: Was John Lewis the chairman at the time?

C: No longer. Stokely Carmichael. Well, he had been the chairman for quite a few years and he was always elected because nobody really cared about being the chairman. When I came into SNCC, the first time I went to one of their staff meetings, they had a vote to elect the chairman. They elected John, went to sleep thinking he's the chairman. But they had a few more votes while he was asleep. He woke up and found out that Stokely Carmichael was the chairman. "What?" "When did this happen?" "While you were asleep." [Laughter]. I knew Stokely and also the people I worked with close to Stokely, so I was on the Stokely side of this change in SNCC.

D: What was that side? What did it represent—

C: Black Power. It was not the Freedom Now side.

D: It was not the Freedom Now side.

C: It wasn't the John Lewis side. In fact, he was very disappointed and he left once he found out Stokely was the chairman and he wasn't the chairman. He left.

D: I see October as a marker of 1966 Black Panther Party is formed. You're in California.

C: No.

D: Not yet?

C: No. I didn't have anything to do with forming the Black Panther Party.

D: No, no, no. I'm saying when did you move to California?

C: When did I move out there . . . ? I went in November—I think it was November.

D: November of [19]66.

C: No. November of [19]67 I think.

D: November of [19]67. Okay. So, what I'm getting at, I'm just trying to keep the timeline going and I'm looking at how you gradually get to organizing at some point with the Black Panther Party and Huey P. Newton campaign.

C: Well, we started it. Newton was arrested in a shoot-out with the Oakland police. He was shot and a policeman was shot, and another policeman was killed and he was arrested and charged with murdering a policeman and wounding another one and he was facing a gas chamber. He wasn't doing much; he was jacked up, you might say. They have a cell at the top of the Alameda County Jail. He was up in this—, so, the Black Panther Party For Self-Defense, that he been a part of, had pretty much collapsed by that time. It had nothing to do with what happened to him. It had to do with the fact that the Black Panthers had planned a demonstration at the state capital. They gone up there because the bill, called Mulford Bill was being debated to change the law that had allowed the Black Panthers or anybody else to openly carry weapons in public. And so, once the Black Panthers, as an organization, did this, the state legislators said they want to change the law that permitted open carrying of weapons 'cus they were fish and game laws, so they didn't like the idea of organized Black group carrying weapons, so they wanted to change the law. And that—that legislation, that negotiation, at the state capitol is something that Bobby Seale brought a delegation of Black Panthers to observe. No one in the delegation knew where to go to observe the state legislature and they asked reporters, who was absolutely flabbergasted to see these twenty-two young men and women with guns, openly carried, walking through this halls of the state legislature. So they sent them to the wrong place. They ended up walking right into the hall, right into the place where the deliberation would happen.

D: Right where it was going on.

C: Right. And the people who were there thought that they came to shoot them or something.

D: Yeah.

C: No, no! This was—excuse me, we are just looking for the observation deck. [Laughter]

D: They walked into the wrong room.

C: They walked into the wrong room.

D: Oh, man. That could have been taken any kind of way.

C: Well, they walked out. But I'm sure none of the state legislators in California had ever seen twenty-two men and women with long guns walking into state legislature.

D: Fully armed.

C: The headlines were rather strange. I think they thought it was an invas—they didn't know what to think and I'll tell you what we found out years and years later when [inaudible 31:02] peoples was making a film about the Black Panther Party. He found out that, the entire state capitol of California, in Sacramento, the entire building, has four capitol policeman. That's just their job to be the capitol police, but twenty-two Panthers came there with weapons to observe, so these capitol police were nowhere to be found. [Laughter] They just disappeared.

D: Four police officers and then—[Laughter]

C: They didn't know what was—

D: It's above their pay grade. Back to the campaign for Huey campaign. What I noticed was that so many times, and that's kinda getting into the gender politics of the party. Women were organizing in ways that don't get a lot of credit.

C: No, no. The Panthers didn't have any gender politics.

D: Nobody under politics.

C: No, they didn't. They didn't even use the term. Men or women could join. It just so happened that more men seemed to join at the beginning. But, that's 'cus a group of men started it like two or three—three men started it. There were women in the group that went to Sacramento. There were women as part of their organization, but they weren't particularly featured. The women who I know who was the first one to actually actively join the Black Panther Party was a woman named Joan Lewis or Matilaba—that was the name she used at the time. She became a member and part of her—she was the same age as one of the high school kids; she knew him. You know, "Can I do this if you're doing it? Can I do . . . ?" "Yeah!" "Can I get a gun too?" [Laughter] It wasn't thought of as an organization that had men and women in, but women came into it and it became one. There were two men that started it. This is a start of an organization, yes.

D: Bobby Seale . . . There is a situation where—, and I think many people, scholars, would attribute the Huey P. campaign to basically give it its resurgence, to pump life back into the organization.

C: Well there wasn't any organization when Huey got arrested. It was collapsed. Bobby Seale was in jail because he had been arrested . . . activities at the state capitol. Huey hadn't gone. He was out. People thought he was a little bit too hot headed to go up to Sacramento, so he was free. But when Bobby was in jail, he was also free. He was left to his own devices. He ended up getting wounded in a shoot-out and then he got, county jail facing death penalty. Bobby was in Santa Rita prison serving time on the Sacramento invasion if you want to call that. That's about the time I came. There wasn't anybody actually leading the party at the point. They had an office that they had lost, so I came out there after Huey was arrested. Eldridge was a parolee; he couldn't travel and he met me in Tennessee. You've got to come out here and help us. I came out there. The first meeting was Eldridge and about four teenagers and me in a room, an empty apartment. He said "We gotta save

Huey. He's in big trouble." He's facing one count of murder and one count of an attempted murder of a policeman. It's like the worse crime. And he's facing the death penalty, and he's Black, and he's the Minister of Defense for the Black Panther Party for Self-Defense.

***

C: It never ends. I just left Oakland for the fiftieth anniversary celebration of the Black Panther Party last week. It doesn't end! It doesn't end. That's what I'm trying to say. People won't let this go. It's fifty years later, and you're asking me about the Black Panther Party.

D: Yes.

C: You weren't even born when it started. No, it doesn't end. That's what I'm saying because I think the conditions that gave rise to the Black Panther Party don't end.

D: Let's talk about those conditions.

C: It's police murder and brutality. It doesn't end. It's illegal but it doesn't end. The target seem to be on Black men. It seems to be their favorite target of police brutality. Sometimes it's Black women. I was thinking about Sandra Bland. How in the world did this woman end up dead? Because she encountered a White, racist, Texas policeman who ended up taking her to jail in the middle of the night. That's how she ended up dead. Now, c'mon. This goes back to—the same kind of things are happening in the 1930s and the 1940s and the 1950s. What is this? 2015 when it happened?

D: Yeah.

C: So it's that dynamic, that dynamic of police violence, police hatred, racism, and all the economic ills that are connected to that. That's why it keeps going on.

D: I saw you participating in the Trayvon Martin rally here.

C: It was in New Haven actually.

D: It was in New Haven actually. We're not too far from there. The shootings that have been happening since Trayvon Martin—there was Eric Garner, or Sandra Bland, or the kid, Tamir Rice. I just wonder if you see any type of solutions that could come about at this point if—

C: Community organizing. It's obvious. People who're organized and who have defense units. These do not happen. These shootings happen in certain kinds of places and certain kinds of times. There are usually people who get isolated and it's obvious that there's a mentality among the law enforcement that it's okay for them to kill Black people because that seems to be what they do. Repeatedly. It's not like every now and then. Particularly Tamir Rice. That's insane. This is a kid, a twelve-year-old. There was an article in the *New York Times* Op-Ed piece by some law students and they said just imagine this. A White twelve-year-old in a park and their neighborhood. Could that kid with a toy gun have been murdered by policemen? Is that conceivable? They said no, it's not conceivable. What makes it conceivable is that it's a kid who's Black in a Black neighborhood with a toy gun. It was pretty obvious the gun was a toy. Anyway, the man, the policeman who shot him didn't even—he saw the little boy and killed him. It's a very short time between the time you saw him and the time he killed him. What does that tell you? This is something about the police mentality, something about the police training, something about the recognition that they are not going to get in trouble for killing a Black kid.

Source: Kathleen Cleaver, Interviewed by Anthony M. Donaldson Jr., November 2, 2016, African American History Project 460, Samuel Proctor Oral History Program Collection, George Smathers Libraries, University of Florida, Gainesville, FL.

2

Reflections on the Black Power Archive

ASHLEY D. FARMER

As a historian of Black women's activism, intellectualism, and radical politics, I am particularly interested in why Black women in the late twentieth century found Black Power to be a productive organizing philosophy and how they shaped it to fit their immediate political needs and long-term emancipatory visions. When I began researching and writing about this question, I was told to think seriously about taking on such a topic because it was doubtful such a study could be completed and this line of inquiry adequately answered. Those who offered up such cautions were not questioning whether or not it was a worthy research pursuit. Instead, the persistent question was: Could I find enough sources in the archives to complete it? Implicit in this query were more insidious questions about whether the artifacts I needed to substantiate claims about Black women's theorizing even existed, let alone if they were formally collected and accessible in a traditional archive. Needless to say, the answer to the question of whether or not I could source this project was not only a resounding "yes" for me but also for the many scholars who have written about the Black Power era before and since.

After all, there is a rich and vibrant Black Power historiography that includes thoughtful first-person accounts from activists such as Elaine Brown and Angela Davis and studies of Black Power icons like Robert F. Williams in Timothy Tyson's *Radio Free Dixie: Robert F. Williams and the Roots of Black Power*. The late 1990s and early 2000s brought rigorous and reflective histories such as Komozi Woodard's *A Nation within a Nation: Amiri Baraka (LeRoi Jones) and Black Power Politics* as well as activist retrospectives including Charles Jones's edited anthology *The Black Panther Party, Reconsidered*.[1] In 2006, Peniel Joseph wove many of these historical strands together in his narrative assessment of the movement, *Waiting 'Til the Midnight Hour.* Since then, historians have authored broader syntheses of the movement. Rhonda Williams, for example, has consolidated narratives about the deep "roots and routes" of the movement in *Concrete Demands: The Search for Black Power in the 20th Century.*[2]

These scholars clearly and persuasively argued what many scholars had already known for years: that Black Power was a viable branch of American and African American history. This proliferation of scholarship, or what Joseph has since called "Black Power Studies," reflects the vibrancy of the movement and the latest innovations in scholarship.[3] In the past two decades, there has been a proliferation of studies that range from overviews of the artistic dimensions of Black Power, such as James Smethurst's *The Black Arts Movement,* to organizational histories such as Joshua Bloom and Waldo Martin's opus, *Black Against Empire: The History and Politics of the Black Panther Party.* Scholars have also assessed the educational and international aspects of the movement. Prime examples include Russell Rickford's *We Are an African People* and Nico Slate's anthology, *Black Power Beyond Borders.*[4] Finally, Black women have become a branch of study all their own within the Black Power historiography with works like Tanisha Ford's *Liberated Threads,* Keisha Blain's, *Set the World on Fire,* and Robyn Spencer's *The Revolution Has Come,* and my own *Remaking Black Power.*[5]

This short survey of the field proves that questions about the ability to source histories about Black women, Black Power, and intellectual history are unfounded. However, it does point to larger conversations about the archives, evidence, and "proof" needed to complete Black Power histories. To some extent, these concerns derive from bias in what scholars decide "counts" as "evidence" of intellectual production during this period.[6] But such debates also speak to long-standing ideas about an imaginary, artificial, and often shifting threshold for having "enough" sources to complete a project. As many scholars implicitly know and have now explicitly stated, we must call into question a "logic of historical methodology" that rests on the perception that there must be enough of the "right" kind of sources in order to make a historical project feasible.[7] Such a standard is especially pernicious when applied to Black history because literacy and racism have mediated and continue to mediate the production and collection of archives. The Black Power historiography proves scholars in this field have moved past such questions about archival "lack." Many find the question of what constitutes "the archive" for this field of scholarship to be a more productive debate.

Indeed, the recent proliferation of Black Power scholarship has made it an important moment for scholars to turn their attention not only to the topical directions of the field, but also to concerns and questions about the collection, organization, storage, and accessibility of archival sources. In particular, it has brought central questions to the fore such as: What is the state of the Black Power archive? How should scholars and archivists conceptualize it? And how should they build archives with a Black Power ethic going forward?

This chapter brings together research on Black Power and archival theory to foreground how scholarship on this era complicates long-held assumptions about archival architecture and collecting practices. Through an analysis of the current state of the Black Power archive, and the power dynamics embedded in archival collection and use, I argue for a reassessment and reconceptualization of Black Power archives as "disorderly distributed," or spread unevenly across multiple geographical, archival, and collecting spaces. The essay speaks to the promise of such a conceptual approach for protecting vulnerable archival collections and bolstering Black Power research. It also calls for integrating Black Power values of accessibility, community control, and self-determination into collecting and processing practices.

The State of the Black Power Archive amid Its Disciplining Structures

Defining and conceptualizing "an archive" is disputed and difficult, as is understanding its constitutive components. Furthermore, demarking its contours, location, and boundaries is not as productive as parsing through the ways in which power operates in the creation and maintenance of archival collections. Nevertheless, a broad working definition is useful. An archive is a collection of physical or digital artifacts cohered around a person, place, group, institution, and/or cause. Included in this definition are those collections that are "formally" processed and publicly accessible as are private, personal collections that are both known and unknown to wider publics and researchers.

Of greater significance is how researchers, historians, and archivists define, interact, and interpret an archive through its traditional processing and disciplining practices. A short survey of Black Power archives amid the foundational ordering regulations of archival collection reveals the limitations of such logics for this era's artifacts. Moreover, the power dynamics embedded in these regulations becomes even more apparent when considered within the context of modern-day repositories and Black Power researchers' experiences within them. Ultimately, an examination of Black Power archives reveals the importance of developing new, more capacious conceptualizations of evidence, artifact, and archive and challenges conventional understandings of the archival experience.

Although contested, one of the central rules of archival collection and arrangement is the *respect des fonds*, a French-designed system in which "all records originating from an administrative authority, corporation, or family would be brought together . . . based on their origins and functions."[8] This principle developed to categorize and preserve a particular type of artifact and prioritizes identifying the origins of artifacts and "locus of their generation."[9] Examples include, but are not limited to, records designed to codify societies, nation-states, and economic systems.

Black Power artifacts often originate from multiple social and political locales and are not always neatly and relationally ordered. More often than not, activists created these artifacts rapidly and in response to an act, event, protest, or moment rather than in an administrative or authoritative capacity. This differs from the origins of many of the first artifacts on which archival collecting and processing rules were based. The politically responsive nature of Black Power archives, along with what might best be described as a Venn diagram of activists and organizations to track, makes it difficult to always identify the origin stories of these archives for the purposes of this type of processing and categorization.

The field's most illuminating evidence also does not fit neatly into the *principle of provenance*, or the archival rule that "stipulates that records originating in one office, agency, or individual must be grouped together and not intermingled with those created by any other office or individual."[10] This is not how most Black Power archives are collected, stored, and catalogued. It would not be productive. Like many other aspects of Black history, such an approach asks our historical subjects to fit into neat categorizations and associations and for archivists to force these artifacts into these confines would be a disservice to the diverse and unconventional ways in which Black Power actors moved and worked.

Other forms of disciplining and gatekeeping come into play beyond collecting and processing measures. Most notably, the lack of diversity and topic expertise among those in the archiving profession often mediates the adequate collecting and processing of minority and marginalized communities' artifacts. As many in the archiving profession have noted, this absence of diverse personnel and training methods is apparent when researchers survey which topics, people, and organizations archivists deem worthy of collection as well as the language used to organize and describe these figures and topics in the finding aid.[11]

Even when archivists collect and process Black Power artifacts according to traditional rules power dynamics shape researchers' review of them. Historian and archivist Randall C. Jimerson offers productive models for thinking about how power flows through archival spaces. Jimerson suggests that archivists and researchers might think about the archive as a temple, a restaurant, and a prison. A temple in the sense that both researchers and archivists view it as a sacred place—one that holds records deemed special and significant and therefore worthy of preservation. In the restaurant metaphor, researchers, hungry for information, go into the archive and choose sources from the finding aid "menu" to satisfy their hunger to create their scholarly dishes. In this metaphor, Jimerson notes, "the researcher remains in the dining room, as a consumer of information, while the most important work of the restaurant takes place out of sight in the kitchen. The reference archivist serves researchers much as the waitress serves restaurant customers" while the rest of the archivists do the work of cooking and designing the "menu" behind the scenes.[12] The prison metaphor foregrounds the regulating and surveillance structures of the archive considering that "the records [in an archive] are imprisoned" but so too "are the researchers, who must consult records in closely guarded chambers under vigilant surveillance."[13]

Black Power historians are familiar with all three frameworks that Jimerson describes. Many have seen how this history can be enshrined in a temple-like atmosphere. A prominent example is the Dr. Huey P. Newton Foundation Inc. collection housed at Stanford University. It is one of the largest collections of Black Panther Party artifacts globally and one that also includes artifacts from many different aspects of the Black Power Movement. The Panthers played and continue to play a predominant (some might say outsized) role in this era and its history. As such, these records are carefully curated, organized, and preserved in one of the country's wealthier universities. Such artifacts are deemed worthy of preservation and validated by their place in a well-known and secure university archive. These collecting practices reify the Panthers as much as they protect their legacy.

Many of the same scholars have also played the role of the diner within the restaurant metaphor. Because an archive devoted entirely to Black

Power is rare, scholars of this period often find themselves treating the finding aid as a menu, selecting boxes and folders and hoping those that they have ordered have the right ingredients for their study. Taking this metaphor a step further, Black Power researchers often locate sources amid what might be viewed as the "à la carte" section of the finding aid: the subject files. Here one might find evidence and artifacts from protests, organizational events, rallies, boycotts, and meetings categorized and organized at the end of the finding aid in alphabetical order—their position on the "menu" an implicit indicator of their perceived importance (or lack thereof); researchers' search for them an index of the desire to create new scholarly dishes.

The growing research on the Republic of New Africa (RNA) reflects this approach. Established in Detroit in 1968, RNA leaders called for a separate nation-state for Black Americans to be created in the southeastern United States and funded through reparations. Even if other Black organizers found the RNA's goals farfetched, they were fascinated with members' analysis and activism and often kept clippings, pamphlets, posters, and primers on the group as members developed and established a national plebiscite in Jackson, Mississippi. Much of this ephemera can be found in the subject files of collections across the country, making for a small, eclectic, and growing body of scholarship on the group.[14]

The archive as a prison for both documents and researchers is perhaps the most palpable metaphor for Black Power scholars. A field dominated by minority researchers and scholars, most Black Power historians recognize that as they work to excavate the artifacts of activists that the state targeted, hounded, and imprisoned, they do so within the "panoptical archive," or one where a guardian keeps these records locked away and watches over the use of them in the reading room.[15]

Take, for example, the FBI Reading Room, which holds voluminous records of the Bureau's Counterintelligence Program or COINTELPRO. These records are crucial to Black Power histories as they offer researchers key details about the threats that activists lived and labored under during FBI Director J. Edgar Hoover's multi-decade attempt to "disrupt and discredit" Black radical groups and their sympathizers. Yet to view many of these documents and reports, scholars have to appeal to the very governmental bureaus that inflicted this harm or go to the source of the surveillance and be surveilled, further subjecting both researcher and subject to carceral logics and government oversight.

Yet even within these uneven power dynamics, archivists and researchers persist in collecting, reviewing, and writing about Black Power and archival resources and repositories are expanding to meet this demand. These collections still lean heavily toward organizational records and the personal papers of male activists and leaders. In addition to the vast archive of the Panthers collected in the Newton files at Stanford, there are now microfilmed collections of artists and organizers such as Amiri Baraka (LeRoi Jones), Robert F. Williams, and Muhammad Ahmad (Max Stanford) that are accessible in multiple libraries across the country. Recently, archivists have begun collecting the records of Black women–centered organizations and activists. The records of Black Power feminist groups, such as the Third World Women's Alliance (TWAA), have now found institutional homes.[16] Some collections, such as activist-intellectual Dr. Gwen Patton's archive, are housed in spaces that reflect their political commitments and communities. Patton's archive is housed at Trenholm State Community College—the location an ode to her familial and organizing roots in Alabama.

Yet there are still large gaps in the collection of Black Power archives. For example, there are few collections devoted exclusively to and organized around Black women activists. Other gaps include prison archives and those of grassroots collectives. These archival omissions are not surprising given that, as Michel-Rolph Trouillot reminds us, the "making of archives involves a number of selective operations" that include the "selection of evidence, selection of themes, selection of procedures" and the inevitable ranking of them.[17] In other words, all archives reflect the power dynamics of society, culture, and the collection biases of those who create and access them and current collections reflect the fact that male-led organizations had and still have the most visibility and value from this period.

It is because of complex web of power dynamics and uneven collecting practices that Black Power scholars' archival approaches have both precipitated and aligned with newer, postmodern understandings of archival collection, organization, and processing. Central to this new conceptualization is the idea that archives are not neutral, a rejection of claims that origin and provenance records must be assigned to a single role or office, and an appreciation for the fact that the order and language that archivists impose on collections is biased.[18] In adopting such an approach, collectors and researchers both implicitly and explicitly further more reflective and capacious understandings of an archive, ones that recognize that "the archivization produces as much as it records the event," and that this has clear implications for how scholars and archivists conceptualize the Black Power archives and evidence.[19]

Moreover, there is now greater recognition of the fact that the claims of archival scarcity that plague Black Power Studies are often due to violence, dehumanization, and erasure in the moment of archival formation. Historians like Marisa Fuentes and Brian Connolly have explored how slavery scholars have to confront violent and silent archives and offer strategies for how to write amid and through the "irretrievably lost . . . desires, fears, and perspectives of many whose enslavement shaped every aspect of their lives."[20] Others such as Saidiya Hartman's have developed strategies such as "critical fabulation." Hartman argues that one way to address archival violence, absence, and what some may call "lack" is to critically "imagine what might have happened or what might have been said or might have been done." She notes that the goal of this approach is not "to give voice" to those who the archive has silenced. Rather, it is a conduit through which students and scholars might "reckon with the precarious lives which are visible only in the moment of their disappearance" in the historical record.[21]

Because of the different, albeit still unfree nature of Black life, and proximity to the period of study, Black Power scholars do not face some of the same challenges as those who study other periods in Black history. To be sure, both violence and silence figure prominently in the formation of this era's archives. However, Black Power scholars are fortunate enough to have records that are not always formed at the moment of disappearance and even, at times, to have access to the subject or creator of the artifact. Yet, many of those who work in this field still share Hartman's investment in exploring the "utopian longings and the promise of a future world that resided in the refusal to be governed" by the prevailing oppressive structures—including archival regulations.[22] Thus, scholars are at a different, but not wholly unrelated, inflection point in interrogating Black Power archives.

Toward a New Understanding of the Black Power Archive

This moment invites scholars, students, and archivists to think about how they might conceptualize Black Power artifacts differently and more productively. One way might be to conceptualize the Black Power artifacts as a *disorderly distributed* archive or adopting an understanding that the evidence of Black Power organizations, ideologies, ideas, approaches, and actors are and should be literally spread everywhere across multiple disjointed and uneven archival spaces. Such a conceptualization helps us understand the peril, promise, and power relationships of the geopolitical arrangement of this era's artifacts. In re-conceptualizing sources as disorderly distributed, one can better understand the skepticism some asserted about a history of Black women intellectuals in the Black Power era. The issue was not that such sources did not exist. It was that their uneven arrangement and geo-spatial spread made such evidence illegible. These discussions reflect the fact that often, the geography of the archive has come to represent the historical actors and ideas themselves. Far too many still frame Black Power actors as unorganized and their theories in disarray because of the disorderly distribution of their artifacts.

Some might ask if the disorderly distribution is the researcher-facing manifestation of a processing backlog. That most repositories have more in their coffers than archivists are able to process is now an established issue across repositories.[23] Yet the uneven distribution of Black Power archives does not simply come from a lack of processing already collected and donated sources; it also stems from a multifactorial process in which a range of actors—including historians—decide what is important to collect from this period. Until relatively recently, both popular and scholarly audiences viewed Black Power as a male-dominated, violent, or even nihilistic part of the Black Freedom Movement. It was the Civil Rights Movement's "evil twin."[24] This framework caused many to initially devalue and overlook these artifacts. In other words, claims about a backlog of Black Power archives rest on the premise that collectors, archivists, and researchers find these artifacts of value, preserved them, and put them in the processing queue in the first place—a feat that is still far too uncommon.

This is not a problem but rather an opportunity for the field. Mirroring the era itself, the disorderly distributed Black Power archive defies the disciplining measures of archival collection and points to productive avenues for artifact organization that can elude or subvert biased processing and collecting practices. It also is an invitation for scholars to conceptualize histories in ways that reflect this defiance. If Black Power asks us to imagine future, freer worlds, then the archive, through its unruliness, compels scholars to think through how to produce scholarship that excavates and appreciates this archival arrangement.

Specifically, the unorthodox arrangement of Black Power archives holds promise for challenging the power dynamics embedded in common conduits of research and knowledge production. Returning to Jimerson's metaphors, the lack of archival concordance embedded in the current distribution of Black Power archives ensures that all records of major organizations and actors are not locked away in a single temple-like repository. Such temples are often built and sustained in spaces like university campuses, which can be fortresses to those who don't "belong" to that particular academic community or area. Black scholars have and continue to pioneer the field of Black Power history. Yet, existing "while Black" in academic spaces has been and remains perilous. One need only look at news reports of Black students and teachers accosted and arrested on college campuses.[25] Because Black Power artifacts are still just as likely to be found in basements, attics, and community centers, away from the gaze of institutional gatekeepers, researchers experience a different type of freedom of movement and engagement in the spaces in which they are collected. A primary goal of Black Power organizing was problematizing power hierarchies, and a non-traditional arrangement of these artifacts furthers this goal of power disruption.

Thinking through the restaurant analogy, the disorderly dispersal of archives fosters Black Power histories that are built on more than one set of records found on one menu or at one "dining" establishment. It also forces researchers to develop new "scholarly dishes" that combine forms, formats, and methodological styles. The lack of ordered collections, and the implicit assumptions of chronology and values that come with them, invites Black Power scholars to be capacious and imaginative in their approaches to histories of this period, and creates the conditions for experimentation and imagination that was at the heart of Black Power activism.

The existing arrangement of the Black Power archive also challenges one of the defining and disciplining structures embedded in this analogy: the finding aid. "Archivists convey provenance information in various parts of a finding aid, which is the final product of archival description," and, as such, engage in a set of determinations and descriptions that obscure and erase different actors from the archive.[26] As former archivist Jarrett Drake suggests, current "collection management tools" and languages are "remnants of a colonized mode of thinking about the world through the gaze of great white men, whose complexities and contradictions could only be explored in the archives by similarly complicated and great white men."[27] One solution that Drake and others pose is that archival descriptions should "reflect the autonomous naming decisions of people and their communities, including and especially if they wish to withhold their names."[28] After all, putting labels and names on acts, events, or ideas, on the finding aid, "set[s] up fields of power" that come to dominate scholarly works.[29] Therefore, it is productive to think through the ways that the disorderly distribution of the Black Power archive both challenges existing naming and categorization biases while also restoring some subjects' dignity, autonomy, and protection. When documents are unevenly distributed, it is more difficult for archivists to create finding aids that order a collection based on hegemonic perceptions or values or to inscribe this history in the repository using oppressive or inaccurate language. This certainty makes some artifacts harder to find. But it also allows scholars to encounter this history on their own terms without preconceived and possibly damaging narratives.

The distribution of the Black Power archive is equally productive for thinking about the architecture of the archival space and the people who inhabit it. Or, to reconsider the idea of the archive as prison. Many Black Power scholars work within traditional repositories. But they also do so amid archival structures that are not designed with inclusivity in mind. There are many pitfalls to "Archiving while Black."[30] This experience was perhaps best captured by famed historian John Hope Franklin. A native of Oklahoma who came of age during Jim Crow, Franklin experienced a series of formative racist incidents that led him to pursue a career in history. In his 1963 essay, "The Dilemma of the American Negro Scholar," he described his efforts to view collections at an archive in North Carolina:

> My arrival created a panic and emergency among the administrators that was, itself, an incident of historic proportions. The archivist frankly informed me that I was the first Negro who had sought to use the facilities there; and as the architect who designed the building had not anticipated such a situation, my use of the manuscripts and other materials would have to be postponed for several days, during which time one of the exhibition rooms would be converted to a reading room for me.

It was never assumed that a Black person would, in Franklin's words, have "the capacity to use the materials there."[31] This issue of capacity was certainly an index of the racist ideas at the time. At the core of this claim, and the alarm over Franklin's physical presence, however, was the fact that neither architect or archivist had conceived of Black people as intellectuals or researchers who would inhabit such spaces. More than half a century later, Black researchers still often have similar experiences in the archive. Many can recount an archivist's sense of surprise upon seeing Black scholars conduct research confidently, clearly familiar with the procedures and regulations. Assuming it is not one of the few repositories dedicated to Black history, employees are sometimes surprised that the archive even houses Black history records and there is confusion as to the importance or significance of these collections.[32]

The lack of traditionally collected and arranged Black Power archives helps minority scholars navigate this dilemma that Franklin first chronicled. Black Power scholars often uncover and work with archives housed in non-traditional spaces such community centers, basements, and dance halls. Imagine the weight that is lifted off the researcher, particularly the researcher of color, in encountering artifacts in this way—away from the panopticon and watchful eyes of staff in the research room; distanced from the added surveillance of being searched upon entering and exiting rooms and buildings. What new possibilities open up for scholars when they can devote their full attention to the archive and the subject rather than balancing research and complying with the unevenly meted out policing procedures of the archive? What new histories can be produced when they encounter archives in community with those who created it, rather than in the sterile light of the reading room?

In this same vein, the disorderly distribution helps undermine the larger veil of state surveillance under which artifacts about Black Power activists were both created and collected. Consider the COINTELPRO records again. For some Black Power actors (women like Audley Moore or Mae Mallory, for example), these records are some of the most complete accountings of their day-to-day existence that researchers have. However, such an archive was forged under the suffocating weight of state surveillance and not at the will or consent of the subject, collector, or processor. Moreover, some who endured COINTELPRO surveillance are still alive today. How then, might a discordant and disorderly distributed archive offer these subjects some of the privacy and protection denied to them in their organizing prime? A fragmented archive might lead to fragmented histories that, in turn, could offer a modicum of privacy and protection for Black Power organizers past and present.

Toward a Black Power Archival Ethic

Just as Black Power advocates have asked us to imagine new worlds, so too does the archive beckon us to develop historical frameworks and collection practices. In defying provenance rules, such sources compel researchers to rethink traditional narratives about the origins, scope, and inclusivity of the movement. Historians' inability to focus or rely solely on the finding aid propels them to come up with new languages, frameworks, and organizational rubrics for telling these stories. The fact that many of these collections lie outside the traditional architecture of the archive calls on researchers to rethink the blueprint from which Black Power history is built. Most importantly, the shape and scope of the Black Power archives asks historians and students of this period to broaden their ideas of what they understand as "archive" and "artifact." Thinking through the archive in this way also asks collectors, scholars, and archivists to be participants in liberation of both the artifacts and the scholarship to which we are committed. The Black Power archive compels us to move away from reinscribing traditional historical tools, frameworks, and disciplining structures when the sources and subjects have and continue to defy them.

This is not a call to wholeheartedly abandon existing archival cataloging and research practices. It is not completely possible to do so. Historians and archivists have and will continue to have to make concessions given the institutional and academic confines. However, focusing on and even perhaps advocating for the continued nature of this disorderly, disobedient, and oppositional collection of the Black Power archives might help more archivists acknowledge the uneven archival terrain in which they work. Furthermore, through actively acknowledging both the geography and the geo-power embedded in archival collections, historians might—much like Black Power organizers—seek to "introduce some dissonance" into their scholarship and offer different interpretations of this historical period based on these collecting imperatives.[33]

As the field proliferates, scholars should begin to ask questions about collection such as: How do we organize artifacts in a way that foregrounds and promotes the political imagination of those it preserves? Is this best done by centralizing these records? Or is the disorderly distributed archive the best approach? If it is the latter, how might we move from an understanding of the disorderly distributed as haphazard to one of unevenly arranged purpose? Just like Black Power organizers, collections that do not adhere to traditional archival rules are more vulnerable. How then, do we ensure that non-traditional archives and collections remain intact while still supporting the liberatory purposes that guide their geo-spatial arrangement? An example of this is Patton's archive housed in a small, historically Black institution in Montgomery, Alabama.[34] A lifelong activist who participated in everything from the Lowndes County Black Panther

Party to anti-Vietnam War organizing, Patton had deep personal and political connections in Alabama. She chose to curate her extensive archive at Trenholm—no doubt as a reflection of her commitments to this community and to local community accessibility. Given that such schools don't receive the same funding, staffing, and grant resources as major universities, one wonders what will come of this wonderful collection and its condition in future years.

For those who publish findings from the archive in one form or another, another set of conversations is equally as important. Editors and historians should consider how collecting and publishing archives in resource books and edited volumes might aid in accessibility. These same collectives might also have more serious conversations about when they choose to not publish certain artifacts for the wider public. Both considerations take on added weight when thinking about government repression, and state-created artifacts and doing the history of the living. Would a set of guidelines about what to ethically publish be productive for scholars in the field? Other questions scholars and collectors might consider is how the scholarship might trend toward subjects collected within the confines of traditional archives and if this is the path they want to continue to support going forward. Finally, how should academics use their positions of power to promote the collection of Black Power archives? Should they advocate for Black Power artifacts to make their way to more formal repositories? Or should they use their power within the academy to promote widely distributed, community-based archives? Such questions will be especially important as we move further into the digital age. What will be the pitfalls and promise of making these archives digitally accessible? How will they document recent activism whose main archive is largely in digital forms today?

Ultimately, historical scholarship provides background and context for the world today. Yet, the best histories show us how to understand the world through a set of questions. Now that the field is in its prime, Black Power scholars can start to pose a set of questions not only about the movement's impact but also about what the artifacts of its actors, subjects, and ideals can tell publics about archival collection and preservation today. At the core of Black Power was an ethic of questioning modes and expressions of power, conversations about naming and power dynamics, ideas about what constituted collectivity and community, and support for new worlds and forms of organization beyond what the state offered Black people every day. Applying these same questions to discussions about Black Power archives and preservation offers a new opportunity to radically rethink the archive and the preservation of Black Power artifacts.

Notes

1. Elaine Brown, *A Taste of Power: A Black Women's Story* (New York: Anchor Books, 1994); Angela Davis, *Angela Davis: An Autobiography* (New York: Random House, 1974); Timothy Tyson, *Radio Free Dixie: Robert F. Williams and the Roots of Black Power* (Chapel Hill: University of North Carolina Press, 1999); Komozi Woodard, *A Nation within a Nation: Amiri Baraka (LeRoi Jones) and Black Power* (Chapel Hill: University of North Carolina Press, 1999); Charles E. Jones, *The Black Panther Party Reconsidered* (Baltimore: Black Classic Press, 1998).
2. Peniel Joseph, *Waiting 'Til the Midnight Hour: A Narrative History of Black Power* (New York: Henry Holt, 2006); Rhonda Williams, *Concrete Demands: The Search for Black Power in the 20th Century* (New York: Routledge, 2015), 4.
3. Peniel Joseph, "Black Liberation Without Apology: Reconceptualizing the Black Power Movement," *The Black Scholar* 31: 3–4 (Fall/Winter 2001): 2–19.
4. James Smethurst, *The Black Arts Movement: Literary Nationalism in the 1960s and 1970s* (Chapel Hill: University of North Carolina Press, 2005); Joshua Bloom and Waldo E. Martin, *Black Against Empire: The History and Politics of the Black Panther Party* (Berkeley: University of California Press, 2013); Russel Rickford, *We Are an African People: Independent Education, Black Power, and the Radical Tradition* (New York: Oxford University Press, 2016); Nico Slate, ed., *Black Power Beyond Borders: The Global Dimensions of the Black Power Movement* (New York: Palgrave McMillian, 2012).
5. Tanisha Ford, *Liberated Threads: Black Women, Style, and the Global Politics of Soul* (Chapel Hill: University of North Carolina Press, 2017); Keisha N. Blain, *Set the World on Fire: Black Nationalist Women and the Global Struggle for Freedom* (Philadelphia: University of Pennsylvania Press, 2018); Robyn C. Spencer, *The Revolution Has Come: Black Power, Gender, and the Black Panther Party in Oakland* (Durham: Duke University Press, 2016); Ashley D. Farmer, *Remaking Black Power: How Black Women Transformed an Era* (Chapel Hill: University of North Carolina Press, 2017).
6. Farmer, *Remaking Black Power*, 15.
7. Marisa Fuentes, *Dispossessed Lives: Enslaved Women, Violence and the Archive* (Philadelphia: University of Pennsylvania Press, 2016), 147; Ashley D. Farmer, "In Search of the Black Women's Archive," *Modern American History* 1: 2 (2018): 289–293.
8. Randall C. Jimerson, *Archives Power: Memory, Accountability, and Social Justice* (Chicago: Society of American Archivists, 2009), 72.
9. Jefferson Baily, "Disrespect des fonds: Rethinking Arrangement and Description in Born-Digital Archives," *Archive Journal* 3 (2013): 201–12.
10. Jimerson, *Archives Power*, 14.
11. Jarrett M. Drake, "RadTech Meets RadArch: Toward a new Principles for Archives

and Archival Description," *On Archivy,* April 6, 2016; Jarrett M. Drake, "Diversity's Discontents: In Search of an Archive of the Oppressed," *Archives and Manuscripts* 47 (2): 270–279.

12 Jimerson, *Archives Power,* 8.
13 Jimerson, *Archives Power,* 6.
14 See, for example: Edward Onaci, *Free the Land: The Republic of New Africa and the Pursuit of the Black Nation State* (Chapel Hill: University of North Carolina Press, 2020); Dan Berger, "'The Malcolm X Doctrine': The Republic of New Afrika and National Liberation on U.S. Soil," in Karen Dubinsky, Catherine Krull, Susan Lord, Dean Mills, and Scott Rutherford, eds., *New World Coming: The Sixties and the Shaping of Global Consciousness* (Toronto: Between the Lines, 2009), 46–55 and Dan Berger with Roxanne Dunbar-Ortiz, "'The Struggle is For Land': Race, Territory, and National Liberation," in Dan Berger, ed., *The Hidden 1970s: Histories of Radicalism* (New Brunswick, NJ: Rutgers University Press, 2010), 57–70.
15 Jimerson, *Archive Power,* 7. For more on the archive as prison, see Eric Ketelaar, "Archival Temples, Archival Prisons: Modes of Power and Protection," *Archival Science,* 2: 3 (2002): 221–238 and Jarrett M. Drake, "Liberatory Archives: Towards Belonging and Believing (Part 1)," *On Archivy,* October 22, 2016.
16 The TWWA's archives are housed at Smith College.
17 Michel-Rolph Trouillot, *Silencing the Past: Power and the Production of History* (Boston: Beacon Press, 1995), 52–53.
18 Terry Cook, "Remembering the Future: Appraisal of Records and the Roles of Archives in Constructing Social Memory," in Frances C. Blouin and William G. Rosenberg, eds., *Archives, Documentation and Institutions of Social Memory* (Ann Arbor: University of Michigan Press, 2006), 169–181.
19 Jacques Derrida, *Archive Fever: A Freudian Impression* (Chicago: University of Chicago Press, 1996), 17.
20 Brian Connolly and Marissa Fuentes, "Introduction: From Archives of Slavery to Liberation Futures?" *History of the Present: A Journal of Critical History* 6: 2 (Fall 2016): 105.
21 Saidiya Hartman, "Venus in Two Acts," *Small Axe* 12: 2 (June 2008), 11.
22 Saidiya Hartman, *Wayward Lives, Beautiful Experiments: Intimate Histories of Social Upheaval* (New York: Norton & Norton Co., 2019), xv.
23 Mark A. Greene and Dennis Meissner, "More Product, Less Process: Revamping Traditional Archival Processing," *American Archivist,* 68 (Fall/Winter 2005): 208–263.
24 Peniel Joseph, "The Black Power Movement: The State of the Field," *Journal of American History* 96: 3 (2009): 752.
25 See, for example: "Library Visit, Then Held at Gunpoint," *New York Times,* January 26, 2015; "A White Student Called the Police on a Black Student Who was Napping. Yale Says It's 'Deeply Troubled,'" *Chronicle of Higher Education,* May 10, 2018.
26 Drake, "RadTech Meets RadArch."
27 Drake, "RadTech Meets RadArch."
28 Drake, "RadTech Meets RadArch."

29 Trouillot, *Silencing the Past,* 115.
30 Ashley D. Farmer, "Archiving While Black," *Chronicle Review,* July 22, 2018.
31 John Hope Franklin, "The Dilemma of the American Negro Scholar," in John Hope Franklin, *Race and History: Selected Essays, 1938–1988* (Baton Rouge: Louisiana State University Press, 1989): 303–304.
32 Farmer, "Archiving While Black."
33 Trouillot, *Silencing the Past,* 58.
34 For more on Patton, see: Gwendolyn Patton, *My Race to Freedom: A Life in the Civil Rights Movement* (New York: New South Books, 2020).

3

"This Is Exactly What's Needed"

An Oral History Interview with Dr. Gwendolyn Zoharah Simmons

Dr. Gwendoyln Zoharah Simmons was born in 1944 and grew up in Memphis, Tennessee, as Gwen Robinson. After her involvement with the sit-in movement at Spelman College, she became a leader in the Student Non-Violent Coordinating Committee (SNCC), the American Friends Service Committee (AFSC), and the National Council of Negro Women. Along with her husband, Simmons briefly joined the Nation of Islam (NOI) from 1967 to 1972. Her experience there and subsequent critique of the NOI influenced her shift into academia, particularly her study of Islamic feminism. Soon, she became a Professor of Religion at the University of Florida, where she worked until retiring in 2019. In the excerpt from two different interviews below, Dr. Simmons traces her personal history from growing up in Memphis to joining SNCC and then embracing that organization's turn toward Black Power. Note: In a few cases, minor errors in the interview transcript have been lightly edited for accuracy or clarity, while small sections were omitted due to the interviews' length. The full text and audio of the interviews are available through the Samuel Proctor Oral History Program archive.

2009 Interview

Matthew Clark [hereafter "C"]: So where and when were you born and what kind of environment did you grow up in?

Gwendolyn Zoharah Simmons [hereafter "S"]: I was born in Memphis, Tennessee, and grew up there and I was born in 1944, August 9th.

C: What was your family unit like growing up?

S: From the time I was three years old, I lived with my paternal grandmother, my father and my grandfather.

C: What was that like?

S: It was wonderful!

C: Okay.
S: My grandmother really was, you know, kind of like my mom. It wasn't that my mom wasn't in the same city. She was. My parents divorced when I was three and my mother had to take a job and my grandmother—paternal grandmother—said, "I'll take care of Gwen while you work." It was supposed to have been temporary, but as it turned out I was living in the house with my grandparents and my dad until I graduated from high school. Even though, you know, I spent weekends with my mom and sometimes in the summer two or three weeks at a time. She was very involved. But my actual residence was with the grandparents and my dad.
C: Was your grandmother a strong figure in your life?
S: Absolutely, very strong, and deeply religious, unlike either of my parents. So that made a big difference I'm sure, as I look back, because religion played such a big role and here I am even teaching religion, right. But my grandmother and grandfather were devout Baptists— went to church all the time. And so that meant I grew up in the church.
C: Okay, were you well off growing up and did you understand whether you were or weren't?
S: Was I what?
C: Well off.
S: Oh no. [Laughter]. No indeed, we were not well off. We were not, you know, homeless or hungry or anything. For that period, I guess I thought—I didn't think of us as poor in that period because my grandfather had a job, my dad had a job. So there were two incomes and my grandmother was a homemaker. So compared to a lot of people in our immediate neighborhood we were better off. But when I think about it now, you know, we certainly weren't middle class but working-class people.
C: Okay. Did your grandmother or your family members ever try to hide segregation from you or did anybody ever talk to you about it?
S: Oh my goodness, they talked about it a lot. It was not hidden.
C: What kinds of things did they say?
S: Well first of all my grandmother, who was born in 1898, had been reared by her grandmother, who had been enslaved. So my grandmother told me the stories that she had been told about slavery. So I knew about slavery from a very personal insight and, you know, my grandparents thought that segregation was very wrong and they talked

about it a lot. And also in my church there was a strong support later for the Civil Rights Movement and all. But yeah, I knew. And then also there was an attempt to protect me also. So that was the other part of it. It was like even though Memphis was urban and claimed to be somewhat civilized, it was still quite dangerous for Black people if you got out of your place. So while I was being taught it was wrong, I was also being taught to stay in my place out of fear of something bad happening to me.

C: Was that how they tried to protect you? By telling you to stay in your place?

S: Yeah, because, you know, clearly if you were attacked or something by a White person, there was almost no chance of anything being done about it legally. And it was interesting: I lived in a little enclave that was all Black. And then in order to kind of get out of the enclave, I had to go through a White neighborhood. Like to get to the buses, the main thoroughfares. We didn't have a car, so I had to walk through. So I was constantly being warned to be very careful, never go through there at night. And sometimes the children would throw rocks at us and call us niggers. So I was very aware of what was happening all around me. And also, interestingly, and we'll get to this later, my grandmother had what I thought was an unnatural fear of the state of Mississippi. And she'd never lived there, so it was totally based on stories. And so it was so interesting that I would later go to Mississippi to work. Because all my growing up she would say, "Never go to Mississippi! It's the worst place in the world for Black people." And she was aware of people who had had to escape from plantations where they worked.

***

C: We talked a little bit about your grandmother and how she was a strong female figure in your life. Do you have any specific stories that you can recall or instances where she would try to protect you or any stories that she told you specifically?

S: Oh my goodness, well, as I told you, she told me a lot about her grandmother who raised her and she told me these Mississippi horror stories. She also told me a lot about sharecropping because that's how she had grown up and how they would work so hard and bring in a good crop and still come out with so little money. So I had heard these stories and she also—she was very bright. She had great desire to go to school beyond the sixth grade, which is where she stopped. Because when she was growing up, there was no beyond the sixth grade in her area and in order for her to go to the seventh grade, eighth, ninth and on, she had to actually go to a boarding school. So she worked so hard to help bring in the crop because her brother had promised her that her money would be hers and she could pay for her tuition. And she had visions of going and finishing high school when the crop came in. Even though she said she had picked so much cotton, just hundreds of pounds, he wouldn't give her her money. And so she never got over that. She talked about it a lot. And that, of course, I later understood why she was so upset with me when I dropped out of college to work in SNCC. It was really that she saw herself living her dream through me. Because I had finished high school. I had done well and I had gotten scholarships, something that was just totally out of the question during her time. So she never forgave me for dropping out of college. But I'm getting ahead of myself. But anyway. [Laughter].

C: That's fine. That's wonderful. Did she push you for education?

S: Oh goodness yes, oh, absolutely. I mean it was never any question. It was like, "You are going to college." "You." It was like I would have let her down if I hadn't done my best. And she was so proud of me and everything at the school requiring any parental involvement. She was just such a push for excellence. The other thing, which also baffled me but I understand now that it had to do with disappointment—she was a registered voter and she was very proud of that. That was a big difference for the Black folk in Memphis. They could register to vote. And she was so proud of her voter registration card. She would be very involved with trying to get out the vote and going from door-to-door during election time and trying to get people to go register and a lot of people said, "Oh, it's not going to do us any good." And she was very active in the church. So at the election time, that would generally be the only time that anybody political—who were all White—would come to the church to get votes. So she would be there taking notes and asking questions. So her civic engagement influenced me. She was also very involved in trying to help the poor. And there were so many poor people. And she was a great gardener and so she taught me gardening. And we had a huge garden and of course we would can food and give food away to the poor and all. So she really—I see her as the great influence of my life. Yeah.

***

C: More about your education, because you received a scholarship to go to Spelman, so you were really involved in school. What was your education like in high school, before college?

S: Well interestingly, I went to school from the first through twelfth grade at the same school, the Manassas High School, and back then they weren't broken out. There might have been a few grammar schools, as they called them, elementary. But I lived close to a very large school and so I went from the first through twelfth grades in the same school. Now we of course had different teachers at different levels. But it was really a very wonderful experience for me, because a couple of people who had had such an impact on my life in the second grade, when I was in the twelfth grade, I could still go and see them, show them my report cards. Because they had such an interest in me for the whole time, from the first through twelfth grade. And there was a real sense of family amongst the school and the students, the teachers. They took a real interest in our lives. So we knew them. Many times they lived in your neighborhood, they went to the same church. And they would get on you if you didn't do well. Almost like your parents. So if you did badly, you didn't want them to know. So it was really amazing and I know that I generally would make the honor society and we had a really strong honor society organization. And they would take us on trips and things. And also when we were studying for tests, teachers would come in early, like seven o'clock in the morning to work with us on whatever it was, English or math. So while the segregated schools, certainly we didn't have the equipment and all that, but the amount of concern and interest that I know I experienced throughout was very affirming and I think had a lot to do with my success.

C: Okay.

S: Yeah.

C: And then you went on to Spelman.

S: I went on to Spelman

***

C: What were your first experiences like in Atlanta and how did they differ from Memphis?

S: Well, when I first got to Spelman I think I thought I had arrived in Heaven. I mean, first of all, it was a beautiful campus. I had grown up, as I said, a working-class family. The neighborhood was run-down and as was often the case in the poor neighborhoods, we didn't have sidewalks. We didn't have paved streets. When it rained, the water backed up and the whole bit. So to go to this—what looked to me like just beautiful, well-manicured lawns and beautifully kept buildings. So I was just totally in heaven. I was so excited. And I liked Atlanta. And Atlanta at that time was considered one of the cities where Blacks had done well. So you had a much larger middle class. One of the things that people did there was take you around to see Black neighborhoods that were upscale, living in beautiful homes with lawns. I remember us doing that right early on and so it was sort of like, "That's how I'm going to live when I finish college and get a good job. That's where I'll live, in one of those brick houses with a beautiful lawn."

C: Was there a heightened sense of awareness of segregation in Atlanta with that upper middle-class community?

S: There was less of that because, first of all, Spelman is a part of something called the Atlanta University Complex. So you had—and still have—not only Spelman, the all women's college, Morehouse the all-men's college, you had the Atlanta University Complex, you had Clark College, you had ITC, which was the Interdenominational Theological Seminary, and you had Morris Brown College. So it was like a real wonderful enclave. Then Hunter Street, which at that time was called Hunter Street, had all these Black-owned businesses, so nice restaurants and pharmacies. So it really kind of shielded you from—and the school really did everything to keep you from going into downtown Atlanta or coming in contact with segregation. That was their way of dealing with it. They really wanted us to stay within those campuses and to do all of our shopping and going out. And then there was a Black theater in walking distance. So they tried to keep us from the downtown—

C: The University tried to protect you.

S: Yeah, they did. I think that must have been happening almost across the board in the Black communities of the South, was to try to protect you. You knew about it. Everybody knew you knew. But it's like, let's live within our own enclave.

2018 Interview

Juliette Barbera [hereafter "B"]: So maybe someone as yourself, who may recall this era of the late 1960s and [19]70s, and maybe even what preceded before then, and what happened after that in terms of what you have observed. Like a firsthand experience of what perhaps Dr. Kendi describes in his book as The Black Campus Movement. You had mentioned in a prior conversation that you had some reflections on observing it. So I just wanted to get your observations. Can you tell us about what you saw on the college campus that you mentioned—I believe it was Temple?

S: Yeah. Well, let me just say that I was a peripheral activist in that particular phase of what I call the long Black freedom movement, which—I'm happy—I got Dr. Kendi's book hoping to have a chance to look at it and only got through the first chapter, which was so eye-opening for me because, of course, he gives in his book on The Black Campus Movement the long history of Black struggle around education. So, I look forward to reading the rest of the book. But, to get back to my own involvement, I think it is important to talk about the movement—the 20th century Civil Rights Movement that evolved into the Black Power Movement. And of course it was during that period that The Black Campus Movement erupted onto the world stage. Certainly the Civil Rights Movement, and the fact that it was the 20th century phase of it, was really initiated by the students sitting-in. College students sitting-in, at a HBCU in North Carolina in Durham—not Durham. What is it? What is it? God. Greensboro. In Greensboro, North Carolina.

***

S: And this is how I initially came into being a part of SNCC. Because as a student activist in Atlanta, as a Spelman college student, I had gotten involved in the sit-ins. And so, in my freshman year, which was in 1962—[19]62, [19]63 was my freshman year. Then [19]63, [19]64, my sophomore year. And I was elected in my sophomore year to be on that Coordinating Committee. Each college that was a part of this sent two representatives to serve on this board, if you will, that helped to make decisions about what SNCC would be doing in the next months and years, it was hoped. And so, of course, once I actually became involved as a member, then I began to understand the inner workings of SNCC and meeting people who had dropped out of school to work full-time. Or, had either graduated in some cases—like John Lewis had already graduated, Stokely Carmichael had already graduated. So not everybody had dropped out, but some had actually graduated and then become full-time workers. Now, speeding ahead to the Black Power Movement after SNCC had helped the local people in Mississippi—the state of Mississippi—organize the Mississippi Freedom Democratic Party as a part of the 1964 Freedom Summer Project. And, let me just add that as a member of the Coordinating Committee—a student at Spelman—I learned of the plans to take up to one thousand college students into Mississippi to work in Mississippi Freedom Summer. And I felt, the more I learned about it—especially after meeting a lot of the organizers from Mississippi—I had to go myself and be a part of that. Anyway, I did go and I was assigned to Laurel, Mississippi, to be the Freedom School coordinator that was one of the three foci of Mississippi Freedom Summer. One was to get as many Black people registered to vote as possible, to start Freedom Schools, and to organize the Mississippi Freedom Democratic Party. So, the party was organized—my town and county was very involved in that. We sent representatives to both Jackson—to the statewide convention—and we also had two people to go to Washington, D.C., as a part of that delegation. Not Washington, I'm sorry. To Atlantic City. To the 1964 Democratic Convention. Our MFDP went to the convention with the plan of supplanting the racist Democratic regulars who had done everything in their power to keep Black people from being involved in the process. And people were stunned that with all of the thousands of people—we had set up a mock registration campaign—since you could be killed in many cases in Mississippi for even trying to register to vote. And so we set up a mock registration campaign so that people who wanted to register to vote, but because they would be killed or lose their jobs, have their houses burned down—participated in our mock registration which we held in churches, beauty and barber shops, at the SNCC offices, called COFO offices, et cetera. And we had collected thousands of registration forms that people had filled out. And these we took to Atlantic City to show to the Credentials Committee that we have thousands of people. Not only Black people, but some White people. And we truly represent the state of Mississippi for the Democratic Party. In spite of that, they sat the regulars and offered a puny two observer seats to the Mississippi Freedom Democratic

Party. And of course the party, led by Mrs. Fannie Lou Hamer and others, rejected two seats as observers. When we got back to Mississippi, many people felt that the democratic process obviously did not work for Black people, even if you played by the rules. And people began talking about—we need other forms of ways of showing our displeasure with the racism and the oppression that we live under. And that you can only gain that through having power. And so the whole idea of Black Power was—it was always there, but it really sort of bubbled up to the top of many people's consciousness. And then, after James Meredith had initiated his March Against Fear and was shot early in that march, as he had set out from Memphis to walk from Memphis to Jackson in defiance of the racism and the violence, and to show Black people that they should register to vote no matter how dangerous it was. That they should not relent from that goal. Anyway, he was shot and seriously wounded. Thank goodness, not killed. And then SNCC people, SCLC people, NAACP people, CORE people, said, "We have to take that march up. We cannot let the violent racist terrorists win." And so they took up the march that Meredith had planned. And in Greenwood, Mississippi, during a rally, Stokely Carmichael of course called out, "Black Power." And all of the young people, and lot of the older people, too—I wasn't there, this is just my hearing about it and all of that. People just loved it and was just enthusiastic over this whole idea of Black Power. So that caught on across the country in the African American community, in spite of the way the media and many of your Black—even Civil Rights leaders— were very upset with that whole idea of Black Power. Needless to say, White people called it reverse racism. They tried to say that SNCC had become like the Ku Klux Klan. I mean, just crazy stuff. But anyway, for the Black community and many allies, they understood that, yes, this is exactly what's needed. So on that, you had that sort of political side of it that began to be seen as organizing for Black Power. And we're talking about electoral power as well as economic power. It never had any violent connotations associated with it. Then, on the other side, so to speak, you had a resurgence of Black consciousness. And this had to do with addressing the years and years—centuries—of racist significations of what it meant to be a person of African descent. And that included everything from your skin, your hair, the shape of your nose, your lips—everything is ugly and detestable, and the only thing that is beautiful is White. And you had the Black Consciousness Movement that arose at the same time that the Black Power idea had caught on. And so then you started hearing, "Black is beautiful." Black women stopped straightening their hair, started wearing naturals, afros. Black people started embracing the whole idea of being an African people, looking into the history of Africa. That Africa is not what we've been taught to believe through the Tarzan movies and all these other movies. That they're cannibals, they have bones in their noses, they're naked, savage beasts, et cetera, et cetera. Which is what we all had been taught. I know that's exactly—having sat through so many Tarzan movies every Saturday, which is when we went to the movies, to the segregated movies. The Tarzan show ran in serial. And so you saw it every weekend. So this is the image that we had of Africa. The only image on the big screen. Not to mention what was being shown to us on the small screens. Amos and Andy, Blackface, Minstrelsy, all of this. So, Black Consciousness along with Black Power rises up in the hearts and minds of Black people across this country. In conjunction with that began the demand for Black Studies. That we have been taught lies and garbage for hundreds of years. And in our schools, even in our historic Black colleges and universities, we don't have African American Studies. We're not even taught the history of Africa or the history of African Americans in the long struggle for justice. So, in this Black student, Black Consciousness, Black Campus Movement, was another part of Black Power and Black Consciousness, and affirmation of our African identity and heritage. This was a part of it. Now, I saw that, I witnessed that. And certainly, at the point that I was peripherally involved was after having left SNCC. Had spent two years working for the National Council of Negro Women in a Black Women's Project. And during my last year in SNCC, in Atlanta, where I was Assistant Director of the Atlanta Project of SNCC, I had met another SNCC organizer named Michael Simmons. And he and I got married while we were in Atlanta. Let me just back up, it's important. He refused to go to Vietnam. And when he got his induction notice, he—along with a number of us—went to the induction center with him and he turned that induction notice in with a letter saying, "I am not going to Vietnam to fight and possibly die for democracy in Vietnam when we do not have democracy here in the US. I have been working for a number of years on getting democracy for Black people and I will continue to do that." He was, of course, charged with draft evasion and was after a number of court cases—he was sentenced to three and a half years in federal prison for being a draft dodger. So, to go back to my chronicle, we—he and I—after being in SNCC, we had gone to Chicago, where I was working as the Midwest Coordinator for the National Council of Negro Women. And then, on a project called Project Woman Power that was organizing women across the US. Black women for social change. And I was the Midwest Coordinator for that. After that project finished, we had moved back to Philadelphia because Michael wanted to go to the Lewisburg Prison to serve his time, because he is a Philadelphian and his parents and brother and close relatives all lived in Philadelphia. So he wanted to be in a prison in the state and Lewisburg was the closest federal prison, so that his family could visit. And therefore we moved to Philadelphia. Back, for him, to Philadelphia. And while he was out on bail, and the SNCC lawyers were trying to get the case overturned—they actually took it to the Supreme Court twice. But the Supreme Court refused to hear the case. So, that kept him on the ground for a few years. And we were in Philadelphia, and Michael had returned to Temple University. He had done two years at Temple and dropped out to work full-time in SNCC. And so he went back to Temple. And when he got there, became very involved with organizing the Black Student Union at Temple. I was a new mother. We had a brand new baby. And I was not a student. So I was a full-time mother and homemaker, so to speak. And Michael was working and also attending Temple and got very involved. I went up there for some of the meetings. I also went up to Temple to join the picket lines and demonstrations that they were having. And often, some of the meetings happened in our home, where they were planning their strategies, et cetera.

Sources: Dr. Gwendolyn Zoharah Simmons, Interview by Matthew Clark, January 15, 2009, AAHP 058A and Interview by Juliette Barbera, December 20, 2018, AAHP 058C, African American History Project, Samuel Proctor Oral History Program, Joel Buchanan Archive of African American History, George Smathers Libraries, University of Florida, Gainesville, FL.

4

The Case for a Black Power Oral History Digital Archive

Jasmin A. Young

The Black Power Movement is still a controversial subject in United States history. The movement arose at a time when warring ideological positions polarized the nation. Black Power activists publicly challenged the country's beliefs, values, and traditions—it was disruptive and bold. Nevertheless, the Black Power Movement has not been incorporated into the narrative framework of our national history. In striking contrast, the stories we tell ourselves about the Civil Rights Movement often feel good. The nation celebrates civil rights heroes such as Martin Luther King Jr. and Rosa Parks. Accolades and applause abound for activists who remained nonviolent in the face of guns, water hoses, nightsticks, and fists, and the nation lauds the passage of two landmark laws—the 1964 Civil Rights Act and the 1965 Voting Rights Act. The Civil Rights fable, as scholar Jeanne Theoharis contends, is bustling with made-for-Hollywood stories about the power of American democracy to overcome all racial evils of the past.[1]

Popular understandings and scholarly framings of Black Power far too often center on leather-clad, gun-toting Black Panthers. Worst, conventional narratives centered on the idea that Black Power undermined racial justice struggles. As Peniel Joseph writes, Black Power is framed "as an unabashed failure and a negative counterpart to more righteous struggles for racial integration, social justice, and economic equality."[2]

The distinction between the Civil Rights and Black Power Movements is significant. Civil Rights and Black Power activism were interrelated yet distinct forms of protest.[3] These two interconnected phases of the modern Black Liberation struggle share many commonalities, including a fundamental goal of obtaining "freedom."[4] Yet, the meaning of freedom and its articulations emerged in historically specific moments and were contested among activists at the time. Each moment or movement had its own set of goals and objectives, set of tactics, cultural norms, ideologies, theorists, discourses, symbols, leaders, and followers. Understanding these differences is vital. As scholars Sundiata Keita Cha-Jua and Clarence Lang remind us, "blurring the distinctions between Civil Rights and Black Power is often the result of a superficial reading of movement tactics, which are presumed to be definitive. Form is mistaken for essence."[5] This essay breaks from persistent trends in African American historiography that conflate Black Power into the vortex of the Civil Rights Movement and frame the Black Power Movement as the impetus for the decline of the Civil Rights Movement.

Moreover, I argue that scholarly and popular views on the Civil Rights and Black Power Movements account for how individuals and institutions funnel financial resources into the former and not the latter. While this is evident in everything from parades to national holidays, it is also evident in the creation of oral history repositories and scholarly resources currently available.

To date, there are over 1533 oral history collections dedicated to the Civil Rights Movement; extensive collections include those located at the Library of Congress, SNCCDigital, UNC-Chapel Hill, Howard, and Wisconsin Universities.[6]

The Black Power Movement, however, has none.

Despite this fact, oral histories have proven to be essential to Black Power Studies; a mere glance at the scholarship reveals oral history sources are foundational to the field.[7]

In this essay, I discuss how essential oral histories are to Black Power Studies, and I offer a brief survey of publicly available oral histories with Black Power activists. I use the remainder of the essay to outline the genealogy of the Black Power Digital Archive (BPDA), a publicly accessible, free, and user-friendly multimedia database of Black Power oral histories. The BPDA has not yet materialized into a website but is an idea in the making, the beginning of which emerged while I was in graduate school. I contend that the BPDA is essential for the future of Black Power Studies.

The Power of Black Power Narratives

The contribution oral history makes to our understanding of the Black Power Movement cannot be overstated. In oral history sources, a researcher can find abundant evidence of the local genesis of the movement, the radicalism of the grassroots base, and the change in the individual and collective consciousness of participants. Oral history can yield evidence rarely available in contemporary written records. For example, interviews reveal why people joined the movement, why they joined one organization over another, and what issues resonated with them most. For instance, Safiya Bukhari's activism began when she pledged a sorority at New York City Community College (now New York Technical College.) As part of her community service, she investigated hungry children in New York City. This investigation introduced her to members of the Black Panther Party in Harlem, and she began working with the Panthers' breakfast program as well as their liberation school.[8] Bukhari eventually joined the BPP and then the Black Liberation Army (BLA) as a commander of an underground collective of revolutionaries.[9] Aside from Assata Shakur, Bukhari is one of the few known female members of the BLA. Without firsthand accounts of Burkhari, we would not know as much about the underground work of the BLA.[10]

Typically participants describe why they joined the movement; these stories connect the individual experience to the larger narrative. But they are also fundamental for challenging common misconceptions, such as the view that the Black Power Movement was a movement for and about Black men. Historian Robyn Spencer's scholarship is apt. She argues that "The Black Panther Party appealed to black women in Oakland who faced issues of poverty and political powerlessness similar to those black men faced and felt the same desire to do something."[11] Spencer's conclusion is drawn from several oral histories she conducted with Black Panther women, including Tarika Lewis, the first young woman to join the Panthers, Elendar Barnes, and Judy Hart. Spencer argues Black women, from as early as 1967, played a principal role in the organization, "asserting leadership and shaping policy."[12]

Researchers concerned with why people joined one Black Power organization over another may also find oral histories particularly insightful. In 2021, Ida McCray explained that she considered joining various organizations, including the Black Panther Party, the Nation of Islam, and the US organization. Like other women, she heard about male-led groups' expectations that female members use their feminine wiles to recruit men, take the "political pipe," a reference to sex, and serve in a secondary or subservient role to male leaders, which concerned her and ultimately influenced her decision.[13] As Rhonda Williams wrote in 2008, "much more historical research remains to be done on women and gender in these types of organizations."[14] I agree, and oral histories will undoubtedly be necessary for that research.

Narrators also describe major moments that spurred them to political action and what factors contributed to their politicization. Oral histories expose nuances in organizational decision-making, shifting ideological positions, or internal conflicts. Often, narrators describe family histories of resistance that affirmed their activism and perceptions of the realities of Black life and the possibilities of liberation.

Family histories of resistance emerge in many narratives of Black Power women. In a 2005 interview conducted by Lorretta Ross, Third World Women's Alliance (TWWA) member Linda Burnham revealed that her parents fostered her political consciousness.[15] She noted, "they had a sort of strong race consciousness from the beginning, and part of that is, it may have been in their own upbringing. My grandmother on my dad's side was a Garveyite . . . [her parents] became exposed to socialists and communists . . . and just because of the politic of the world at that time, ideas of liberation were linked to ideas of bringing to bear a socialist world."[16] Her parents, Dorothy Challenor Burnham and Louis Everett Burnham, were members of the Young Communist League in the 1930s and 1940s, which was fertile ground for Linda's future political activity, ". . . basically I grew up in a highly political family," she declared.

Likewise, Dara Abubakari (Virginia Collins) also revealed in a 1979 oral history that she came from a "real radical" family.[17] Her parents were members of the NAACP, and her dad was a devout follower of Marcus Garvey. Much like her father and mother, Abubakari grew to become a lifelong activist.[18] Her political identity was wrapped up in Garveyism and Pan-Africanism; she exclaimed, "Oh yeh, Oh yeh' I'm a member; I call myself a tail-end member, but during Garvey time, Poppa and them was members."[19] Abubakari joined the Provisional Government of the Republic of New Africa (PGRNA), founded in 1968 in Detroit. The RNA advocated the creation of an independent territorial nation for people of African descent. The new Black territory included the lands of Louisiana, Mississippi, Alabama, Georgia, and South Carolina.[20] Members of the Black nation renounced their US citizenship and reclaimed, renamed, and asserted themselves as "New Afrikans," members of the RNA. Abubakari's evolution as an activist, proponent of self-defense, and Black freedom fighter were all rooted in a tradition that began with her family.

The case of Linda Burnham and Dara Abubakari tells us that family histories of resistance are a significant component of understanding Black Power activists and why women joined certain organizations. Drawing on Stephen Berrey's work, I argued elsewhere that Black families, including parents and relatives, functioned as critical institutions for planting the seeds of subversion.[21] Early life experiences shaped young girls' perceptions of activism. Linda Burnham was born on January 9, 1948, in Brooklyn, New York. She was in her early twenties when she joined the Black Power Movement. Abubakari, on the other hand, was born in Plaquemines Parish, Louisiana, in 1915. When the PGRNA was formed, she was in her fifties. While age may not have been a determining factor in whether women participated in the Black Power Movement, there is evidence—oral histories—to suggest that family histories of resistance did play a role in whether women participated and how.

Black Power Collections

While oral histories exist and are available to the public, there are several issues to consider. First, not all interviews are transcribed or open to the public. Second, some oral histories conducted with Black Power activists are labeled and or cataloged in Civil Rights collections, making it difficult for researchers to locate much-needed sources. The distinction here is significant; while some Civil Rights activists were also Black Power activists (Stokely Carmichael is a brilliant example), not all Black Power activists have their roots in the Civil Rights Movement. Greater distinctions and clarity here and in the scholarship is necessary. Third, the focus of collections varies: Some smaller collections are focused on an individual person. In contrast, others are locally oriented or focused on a specific organization or chapter of an organization. The list of collections in this essay is by no means complete.

Overwhelmingly, researchers find Black Power oral histories in Civil Rights collections and repositories. The Ralph Bunche Oral History Collection (Civil Rights Documentation Project) at the Moorland-Spingarn Research Center at Howard University is one of the largest and most diverse oral history projects. The collection contains over seven hundred interviews conducted between 1967 and 1971, and these real-time interviews are available digitally through Archives Unbound–Gale. But some narrators in this collection were squarely in Black Power organizations. For instance, the collection has an interview with Ernie Allen, co-founder, and editor of *Soulbook*, a Black revolutionary journal. Allen was a University of California at Berkeley transfer student from Merritt College who was active in the Afro-American Association (AAA). Both the Black Panther Party for Self-Defense and the US Organization have their origins in the AAA.[22] To conflate this subject/organization with the Civil Rights Movement is problematic because it distorts the importance of these two distinct eras. Similarly, the Civil Rights History Project Collection, 2010–2016, created by the National Museum of African American History and Culture, has filmed over 108 oral history interviews with "participants of the Civil Rights Movement."[23] But again, some interviews are with Black Power activists. In fact, Black Panther Party members are included in this collection, including Kathleen Cleaver, Norma Mtume, Erika Huggins, and Roberta Alexander—some of these narrators were not "participants of the Civil Rights Movement." Interviews with Black Power activists placed in Civil Rights collections should inspire scholars to revisit key debates in the field of Black Power Studies. With some scholars conflating Black Power with Civil Rights, we must reconsider the debates about the chronology of the movement, its contours, precursors, how to define the Black Power Movement, and its participants.[24] These questions are all still relevant today.

Scholars interested in more localized evidence have a few options, including the Black Power Archives Oral History Project at California State University, Northridge, and the Washington D.C. Black Power Chronicles. The Tom and Ethel Bradley Center at California State University, Northridge, features oral histories of Black Power activists in the Los Angeles area. The collection contains some sixteen visual interviews with movement participants available through its YouTube channel.[25] Narrators include members of the Black Panther Party for Self-Defense Southern California Chapter (BPP), the US organization, Che-Lumumba Club, Community Alert Patrol, and SNCC-Los Angeles. Although the project is active and ongoing, many of the interviews have not been transcribed, and some will not be available to the public until after the narrator is deceased.

Promisingly, activists are also leading the charge to collect and conduct interviews and preserve the history of the Black Power Movement. In 2015 the SNCC Legacy Project created the Black Power Chronicles (BPC) to address the historical absences of the Black Power Movement.[26] According to the website, the BPC has two specifics aims:

Identify and commemorate the 50th anniversary of the call for Black Power on June 16, 1966, and thereby establish it as a significant historical event that deserves to be remembered and studied by people throughout the world; and

Undertake a grassroots organizing campaign to uncover the stories and insights about the Black Power era (1966–1998) as told by Black Power veterans who worked in their communities to build new programs and institutions across the country.[27]

The Black Power Chronicles Oral History Committee videotaped interviews with 29 Washington D.C. activists, artists, political leaders, and scholars.[28] This collection offers researchers a localized perspective of Black Power in the nation's capital and features interviews with Courtland Cox, Jennifer Lawson, and Dorie Ladner. The DC oral histories focus on various aspects of the Black Power Movement. For instance, researchers interested in Black Power institutions may find the founding of Drum and Spear Bookstore and Press insightful. The store's leadership included Cox, Ralph Featherstone, Charlie Cobb, and Judy Richardson, all former SNCC organizers. They envision Drum and Spear as an important politicizing tool for the Black Power Movement. Richardson recalled in a 1994 interview, "Africans at home and abroad . . . African diaspora . . . what we were trying to build was a sense of solidarity . . . That's what these bookstores were about, they were revolutionizing the Black mind. They were opening it up in a way then that anything was then possible."[29]

Organizational collections also exist primarily for the Black Panther Party, but not the Black Power Movement as a whole.[30] The Seattle Civil Rights and Labor History Project at the University of Washington has over eighty oral histories with activists, sixteen of which are with members of the Black Panther Party, Seattle chapter, including co-founders Elmer Dixon and his brother Aaron Dixon.[31] The videotaped oral histories are accompanied by hundreds of photographs, documents, and a full transcript of the 1970 Congressional Hearing investigating the Seattle BPP chapter. Localized studies are significant, particularly in national organizations where chapter history added important nuance to the national story—oral histories connect the local to the national.[32] The strength of this collection also lies in the diversity of perspectives represented in the interviews. Kenyatto Amen-Allah describes attending the BPP's liberations school, and Shamseddin Williams's father was a Panther. In his narrative, he offers insights into the BPP's community programs for children. Scholars interested in Black Power's children would find these sources useful.[33]

"Not Just a Housewife": My Search for Mabel Williams

Oral histories have been pivotal to my research as well. My current research centers on Black women and armed resistance in the Civil Rights and Black Power eras. The project was birthed from a research paper I worked on as a graduate student in the Department of History at Rutgers University, New Brunswick. The seminar paper examined the activism of Mabel Williams, a vocal proponent of armed self-defense and a member of the National Association for the Advancement of Colored People (NAACP). Although she is most commonly known as the wife of Robert F. Williams, she "was not just a housewife."[34] The Monroe chapter of the NAACP worked to integrate public facilities, including the local public library, school, and swimming pool. These efforts energized the Ku Klux Klan. Frequently, newspapers advertised KKK rallies, and attendees ranged from a few hundred to several thousand. On far too many occasions, demonstrations turned into motorcades through the Black section of Monroe, where joyriders shot firearms into the air and terrorized the community. Mabel and Robert regarded these actions as violent and sought the help of city officials. But law enforcement refused to stop the Klan. In response, Mabel and Robert formed a protective unit in Monroe, the Union County Rifle club, in 1957 to protect their homes and their community.[35] Two years later, Mabel, Robert, and their friend Ethel Azalea Johnson created the *Crusader* newsletter. The paper's purpose was to win national support for the Monroe movement and promote armed self-defense. Under her guiding hand, the publication went from a local NAACP branch newsletter, sold on the street of Monroe for ten cents, to a weekly with a national and international readership.

Despite Mabel's very active role in the Monroe movement, most Black Power scholarship centers on Robert F. Williams as a one-man show.[36] Based on the twenty-six microfilm reels of Robert Williams's archive, I knew there was more to the story.[37] But the papers offered scant glimpses of Mabel's political philosophy and commitment to liberation—aspects of her political life I was most interested in examining. I never found the gems I hoped to find; she was lost in her husband's archive.

I used the few existing oral histories with Mabel to construct a paper about her activism and contribution to Black Power.[38] But to truly get at the information I was seeking; I knew I needed to talk with her. I phoned my contacts to get her information and successfully acquired her home phone and mobile number. I called several times, but no one returned my calls. I ended the semester having not spoken to Mabel but used sources from the archive to complete the seminar paper.

As my dissertation project crystallized, I knew Mabel Williams would be a part of the work—and I knew I needed to talk with her. At the time, she was in her early eighties, and time was precious. My contacts repeatedly urged me to move fast, "she isn't doing well," they warned. I periodically attempted to phone her over the semesters to no avail. I knew there was more to be discovered.

My fourth year as a graduate student finally brought the breakthrough I sought. The Wright Museum in Detroit held a "Liberation Film Series" that would feature "Negroes with Guns," a documentary focused on Robert F. Williams. Following the screening would be a conversation with Mabel Williams on "The Right to Black Self-Defense against Human Injustice & Oppression." The panel included their son John Williams and two other activists, General Baker and Gloria House. I decided I would go to the screening and introduced myself to Mabel. I jumped in the car with my friend and drove to Detroit in wintery weather for ten hours.

Activists, scholars, students, and Detroit residents packed the auditorium. Mabel arrived late. The MC introduced her as "Robert F. Williams's widow" and said nothing about her practice of armed self-defense. This was precisely the type of narrative I wanted my scholarship to push against. The film began, and I sat impatiently waiting for my chance. Little did I know someone had ushered Mabel out before the movie ended. She did not sit on the panel afterward, nor was she available for Q&A. I had come so far and tried for so many years to contact her—it was devastating. The silver lining was my new connection to her son, John Williams, the gatekeeper. He gave me his direct number and promised we would talk once I returned to the east coast.

I called immediately, and we talked for over an hour. I listened as John offered his perspective on his mother's political organizing, commitments, and beliefs. But he was very young when they lived in Monroe.[39] Still, my resolve had not wavered; my intention to conduct an oral history with her was still at the forefront, although I knew it was essential to establish trust and credibility with him. He was also resolute. His mother was not doing well and may not be up for talking. We agreed to speak again; he would pass along some preliminary questions to her and even hinted at potential papers, writings, speeches, a memoir, and documents in their family home belonging to Mabel. I, of course, hoped to see them.

On April 19, 2014, Mabel Williams passed away in Detroit, Michigan, quietly, without much fanfare. She did not complete her memoir as she had hoped. And only a handful of scholars have written about her activism.[40]

My search for Mabel Williams inspired me to create the BPDA. It also offers critical insights into the challenges of researching Black Power and Black women. I had hoped to record Mabel's voice in an effort to circumscribe the silences in the archive and to preserve her account of history. Her passing underscores the urgency researchers must have in preserving the voices of Black Power activists and Black Power women especially. It also points to the importance of existing oral histories of Black Power activists. Without hearing Mabel Williams's voice, we would certainly believe the worn-out trope that Robert F. Williams was a one-man show.

The Need for a Black Power Digital Archive

There is no oral history collection or repository oriented toward the Black Power Movement as a national effort that combines various narrators from various organizations, affiliations, and locations. The dearth of oral histories on Black Power activists inspired me to create a BPDA. While still in the ideation stage, I envision the BPDA website as a user-friendly, free multimedia digital humanities database that provides Black Power interviews to researchers as well as teachers, students, journalists, activists, and the public. Over the next several years, I will collect, conduct, preserve, and digitalize oral histories of Black Power Movement participants. The BPDA will offer text, audio, and visual recordings of oral histories of people who participated in the Black Power Movement from 1965 to 1985. I describe the BPDA in detail below, noting how such a resource could be used in new directions of Black Power Studies in the future.

The BPDA project is essential for three reasons: (1) It creates a publicly accessible, free, and user-friendly curated online collection. (2) A project of this magnitude would allow scholars across the disciplines and interdisciplinary fields, including Political Science, Sociology, History, Gender Studies, Africana Studies, Anthropology, and more to conduct path-breaking research with new primary sources. (3) It broadens the public knowledge about US History, Black History, and Women's History, which is instructive for understanding how Black Power offered a set of alternative political imaginations of resistance and nation-building, not least of all on healthcare, reproductive justice, welfare, labor, anticolonialism, and education.

The likely audience for this website and resource also illuminates its utility and necessity. Indeed, scholars will benefit from the BPDA and find this valuable information for doing their research. The website will appeal to students (undergraduate and graduate), public historians, archivists, librarians, and museums. Additionally, a non-scholarly audience will be interested in this site, including politicians, activists, community centers, organizers, and artists interested in sources, events, and themes from the Black Power Movement.[41]

The project comprises several phases. The first phase consists of launching the BPDA website, which details existing publicly assessable oral histories. Future phases of the work involve conducting interviews with Black Power activists and participants in the movement. Of primary concern is conducting interviews with activists, many of whom are aging and in their late 60s and early 70s. Activists are willing to tell their stories now more than ever. They are willing to sit for an interview; there is a sense of urgency in recording their narratives. Since Mabel Williams passed away, several other Black Power activists have transitioned without public oral histories recorded. On January 30, 2019, Nehanda Abiodun passed away in Havana, Cuba, where she lived in exile since the 1990s.[42] Abiodun spent her twenties as an activist in Harlem, New York. She worked with other revolutionaries using acupuncture to address drug addiction in the Black community at the Lincoln Detox center in the South Bronx. Abiodun was also a member of the BLA and PGRNA and was wanted in the United States on charges related to clandestine revolutionary activity. For researchers interested in the connections between health care, acupuncture, and radical politics, an oral history of Abiodun would have been essential.[43] Training students to conduct oral histories with Black Power activists is also important for this project and for teaching Black Power to future generations.

To be clear, there are several other factors to consider when embarking on oral histories with Black Power activists, particularly around their safety. Like Abiodun, other activists have lived in exile or under government surveillance with the threat of a US government attack for decades. This reality presents certain difficulties with preserving narratives that may incriminate or endanger. The harassment, rearrests, and arraignment of the San Francisco 8 on trumped-up charges with no new evidence thirty years after the alleged crime is only one example.[44] The two-million-dollar bounty for Assata Shakur (as of May 2013, she was added to the FBI Most Wanted Terrorist List) is another. Despite these realities, activists understand the importance of preserving their history through their narratives. They understand the time is now.

The third stage involves an extensive mapping project hosted on the website. The maps will reveal the geographical landscape of the Black Power Movement: cities where significant events transpired. For instance, the 1972 National Black Political Convention in Gary, Indiana, the murder of Fred Hampton and Mark Clark in Chicago, and Wattstax in Los Angeles, California; as well as lesser-known moments such as the organizing efforts of the Combahee River Collective in Boston, Massachusetts, as they fought to combat sexual-violence against Black women in the wake of the serial murders of twelve Black women. The maps will show historic images combined with local histories of the Black Power Movement.[45]

The BPDA will allow users to examine the Black Power Movement through various indexing tags. These tags uncover the interconnected continuum and consociation of Black Power. The rich, complex, and nuanced history of the movement will be evident through the various descriptors— gender, organizations, geography, political ideology, causes, major events, etc. Immersed within the categories are critical insights into the Black Power Movement, revealing a multitude of historical interventions. The benefits of such an archive are plentiful. When we examine activists across organizations, surrounding key events, and in specific cities, it changes what we think we know about the Black Power Movement. When we consider the future of Black Power Studies, we must account for how various actors moved across organizations, evolved their political identities, collaborated on common goals, organized together in local spaces, and conceived of a new world. A platform that places narratives in context with one another allows us to ask new and innovative questions. For instance, when we think of the Black student movement, we may consider how Black student protesters collaborated from different schools in the same area. A search of "Black student movement" and "New York City," for instance, would yield oral histories from students at various institutions: Columbia University, Hunter College, and City College.[46] Similarly, the same search with "Los Angeles" would reveal how students at various colleges shared resources, discussed tactics, and found common ground on campuses of higher education and K-12 schools in the LA area.

Oral histories will recover the role of local people in the Black Power Movement and shed new light on the relationships between local, state, and national actors. It can provide fresh insights into collaborations, conflicts, and everything in between—all grounded in the lived experiences of the grassroots organizers and participants in the Black liberation struggles. Finally, the BPDA will be a joint effort among scholars, students, and activists to preserve the history of the Black Power Movement. When I reflect on the importance of the Black Power Movement and its goals, I consider the lessons we can learn from the past. And how those lessons can help us address our contemporary issues. The mission of the BPDA will be to teach students, independent scholars, and community organizations about the Black Power Movement, and how to build on the legacy Black Power activists left. Oral histories continue to be an essential source for scholars interested in the Black Power Movement, we must preserve the history of the movement for there to be a future in Black Power Studies.

Notes

1 Several scholars have discussed the ways the Civil Rights Movement has been a part of nation-building and mythmaking for the United States. See, for instance, Jacquelyn Dowd Hall, "The Long Civil Rights Movement and the Political Uses of the Past," *The Journal of American History* 91, no. 4 (2005): 1233; Jeanne Theoharis, *A More Beautiful and Terrible History: The Uses and Misuses of Civil Rights History* (Beacon Press, 2018).
2 Peniel E. Joseph, "The Black Power Movement: A State of the Field," *The Journal of American History* 96, no. 3 (2009): 752.
3 See Chu-Jua and Lang for a well-articulated critique of the Long Movement thesis that has joined Civil Rights and Black Power together, pushing the temporal boundaries of the dominant narrative, but obscuring the differences between these two waves of the Black Liberation Movement. Cha-Jua and Lang, "The 'Long Movement' as Vampire." Although not a new concept, Hall's article most poignantly articulates the "Long Movement" thesis. Hall's article is especially useful for considering the political (mis)uses of the dominant Civil Rights Movement narrative, particularly by right-wing conservative politicians, neoliberals, and scholars. Hall, "The Long Civil Rights Movement and the Political Uses of the Past"; Also see Theoharis, "Black Freedom Studies"; Theoharis and Woodard, *Freedom North*; Payne, *Groundwork*; Joseph, "The Black Power Movement"; Joseph, *Waiting 'Til the Midnight Hour*; Joseph, *The Black Power Movement: Rethinking the Civil Rights-Black Power Era*.
4 I borrow the concept of the waves from Vincent Harding. In *There is a River: The Black Struggle for Freedom in America*, historian Harding uses the metaphor of a river with many currents to symbolize the diverse ideologies informing Black resistance struggle. Harding argues that, by the beginning of the 18th Century, "many basic currents in the black river had been formed." He identifies the emergence of three major currents, namely: survival; protest and resistance; and radicalism

(which includes forms of revolutionary struggle and armed revolt.) Black people's experience in the US was not only one of oppression but also a history that bears witness to a continuum of individual and collective resistance. This continuum, or movement toward liberation, has always consisted of many different impulses. Harding, *There Is a River;* also see Carson, "Civil Rights Reform and the Black Freedom Struggle"; Theoharis, "Black Freedom Studies."

5 Cha-Jua and Lang, "The 'Long Movement' as Vampire," 276.
6 On May 12, 2009, the US Congress directed the Library of Congress (LOC) and the Smithsonian Institution's National Museum of African American History and Culture (NMAAHC) to conduct a survey of existing oral history collections with relevance to the Civil Rights Movement. The survey database was completed in 2011 and can be accessed at http://www.loc.gov/folklife/civilrights/survey/index.php. "About This Collection—Civil Rights History Project—Collections," web page, Library of Congress, Washington, D.C. 20540 USA, accessed August 27, 2015, http://www.loc.gov/collection/civil-rights-history-project/about-this-collection/.
7 See, for example, Charles E Jones, ed., *The Black Panther Party (Reconsidered)* (Baltimore, MD: Black Classic Press, 2005); Tracye Matthews, "'No One Ever Asks, What a Man's Place in the Revolution Is': Gender and the Politics of the Black Panther Party, 1966–1971," in *The Black Panther Party Reconsidered,* ed. Charles E Jones, 1998, 267–304; Scot Brown, *Fighting for Us* (NYU Press, 2005); Joseph, *Waiting 'Til the Midnight Hour;* Ibram Rogers, "Remembering the Black Campus Movement: An Oral History Interview with James P. Garrett," 2009, 12; Donna Murch, *Living for the City: Migration, Education, and the Rise of the Black Panther Party in Oakland, California* (UNC Press, 2010); Ibram X. Kendi, *The Black Campus Movement: Black Students and the Racial Reconstitution of Higher Education, 1965–1972* (New York: Palgrave Macmillan, 2012); Akinyele Omowale Umoja, *We Will Shoot Back: Armed Resistance in the Mississippi Freedom Movement,* 2013; Robyn C. Spencer, *The Revolution Has Come: Black Power, Gender, and the Black Panther Party in Oakland* (Durham: Duke University Press, 2016); Angela D. LeBlanc-Ernest, "'The Most Qualified Person to Handle the Job': Black Panther Party Women, 1966–1982," in *The Black Panther Party Reconsidered,* ed. Charles E Jones, 1998, 305–34; Ashley D. Farmer, *Remaking Black Power: How Black Women Transformed an Era* (Chapel Hill: University of North Carolina Press, 2017); Jonathan Fenderson, *Building the Black Arts Movement: Hoyt Fuller and the Cultural Politics of the 1960s* (Urbana: University of Illinois Press, 2019); Curtis J. Austin and Elbert "Big Man" Howard, *Up Against the Wall: Violence in the Making and Unmaking of the Black Panther Party* (Fayetteville: University of Arkansas Press, 2008); Jakobi Williams, *From the Bullet to the Ballot: The Illinois Chapter of the Black Panther Party and Racial Coalition Politics in Chicago* (Chapel Hill: University of North Carolina Press, 2013).
8 Safiya Bukhari, WW Interviews Safiya Bukhari, interview by Imani Henry, Transcript, n.d.
9 Interview with Safiya Bukhari distributed by Arm the Spirit, Transcript, September 27, 1992, http://whgbetc.com/mind/bpp-safiya-bio.html.

10 A handful of scholars have examined the underground aspect of the Black Power Movement. See Akinyele Omowale Umoja, "Repression Breeds Resistance: The Black Liberation Army and the Radical Legacy of the Black Panther Party," *New Political Science* 21, no. 2 (1999): 131–55; Joy James, *Imprisoned Intellectuals: America's Political Prisoners Write on Life, Liberation, and Rebellion* (Rowman & Littlefield Publishers, 2004); Gaidi Faraj, "Unearthing the Underground: A Study of Radical Activism in the Black Panther Party and the Black Liberation Army" (Ph.D., United States—California, University of California, Berkeley, 2007).
11 Spencer, *The Revolution Has Come*, 46.
12 In addition to her book, also see Robyn C. Spencer, "Engendering the Black Freedom Struggle: Revolutionary Black Womanhood and the Black Panther Party in the Bay Area, California," *Journal of Women's History* 20, no. 1 (2008): 90–113.
13 These expectations were not universal nor universally expected of all women. More importantly, women within these organizations had varying degrees of power, access, and status. Interview with Ida McCray, March 2021, In author's possession.
14 Rhonda Y. Williams, "Black Women and Black Power," *OAH Magazine of History* 22, no. 3 (2008): 23.
15 The TWWA believed that the goal of the Black Power movement should be to seize state power from the white capitalist ruling class. Their position had much in common with other revolutionary organizations, but their feminist emphasis on Black women's engagement in armed struggle differentiated them from other groups. Jasmin A. Young, "Strapped: A Historical Analysis of Black Women and Armed Resistance, 1959–1979" (PhD Thesis, Rutgers University-School of Graduate Studies, 2018); Also see Stephen Ward, "The Third World Women's Alliance: Black Feminist Radicalism and Black Power Politics," in *The Black Power Movement: Rethinking the Civil Rights-Black Power Era*, ed. Peniel E. Joseph (Routledge, 2006); Patricia Romney, *We Were There: The Third World Women's Alliance and the Second Wave* (Feminist Press at CUNY, 2021).
16 Linda Burnham, interview by Ross, Loretta J., Transcript, March 18, 2005, Voices of Feminism Oral History Project, Sophia Smith Collection, Smith College.
17 Glenda Stevens, Virginia Collins interview by Glenda Stevens, August 31, 1979, Box 1 Folder 17, Roger-Stevens Collection Amistad Research Center.
18 See Ashley Farmer's essay on Collins (Abubakari), one of the few scholarly treatments to date. Ashley D. Farmer, "Mothers of Pan-Africanism: Audley Moore and Dara Abubakari," *Women, Gender, and Families of Color* 4, no. 2 (2016): 274, https://doi.org/10.5406/womgenfamcol.4.2.0274.
19 Stevens, Virginia Collins interview by Glenda Stevens.
20 The new government's leadership included luminaries such as Robert F. Williams, who served as the President in exile; Betty Shabazz, widow of Malcolm X, who served as Vice President; and Queen Mother Moore, who functioned as the Minister of Health and Welfare. Abubakari was named one of the Vice Presidents of the organization. It was at this point she changed her name to Dara Abubakari, an act of self-determination. Umoja, *We Will Shoot Back*, 186–91.

21 Stephen A. Berrey, "Resistance Begins at Home: The Black Family and Lessons in Survival and Subversion in Jim Crow Mississippi," *Black Women, Gender + Families* 3, no. 1 (2009): 66.
22 MSRC Staff, "Ralph Bunche Oral History Collection," *Manuscript Division Finding Aids,* October 1, 2015, https://dh.howard.edu/finaid_manu/171.
23 According to the website, the United States Congress authorized a national initiative by passing the Civil Rights History Project Act of 2009. The law directed the LOC and the Smithsonian Institution's NMAAHC to record interviews with people who participated in the Civil Rights Movement. "Database—The Civil Rights History Project: Survey of Collections and Repositories (The American Folklife Center, Library of Congress)," accessed April 6, 2022, https://www.loc.gov/folklife/civilrights/survey/index.php.
24 See Jones and Umoja's critique about conflating Civil Rights with Black Power Charles E. Jones and Akinyele Umoja, "Black Power Studies," in *Black Power Encyclopedia,* ed. Akinyele Umoja, Karin L. Stanford, and Jasmin A. Young (Santa Barbara, California: Greenwood, 2018).
25 Tom et al., "Black Power Archives Oral History Project," California State University, Northridge, November 10, 2021, https://www.csun.edu/bradley-center/black-power-archives-oral-history-project.
26 The SNCC Legacy Project's mission centers on the idea that SNCC stories need to be told and interpreted by SNCC veterans themselves. The BPC includes activists Karen Spellman, Dorie Ladner, Joyce Ladner, Gaynelle Henderson, Courtland Cox, Sylvia Hill, Jennifer Lawson, Nkechi Taif, and many others. "About Black Power Chronicles | Black Power Chronicles," accessed April 6, 2022, https://blackpowerchronicles.org/about-black-power-chronicles/.
27 "About Black Power Chronicles | Black Power Chronicles."
28 The videos are available via YouTube. There are no transcriptions or tags for the interviews. "DC Oral Histories | Black Power Chronicles," accessed April 6, 2022, https://blackpowerchronicles.org/dc-oral-histories/.
29 Colin Beckles, "Black Bookstores, Black Power, and the F.B.I.: The Case of Drum and Spear," *The Western Journal of Black Studies* 20, no. 2 (Summer 1996): 65.
30 While the BPP was the era's most iconic organization, each chapter was different, and its member's experiences varied. Collections on individual chapters are necessary but still do not satisfy the need for a robust Black Power Movement Collection.
31 "Activist Oral Histories—Seattle Civil Rights and Labor History Project," accessed April 6, 2022, https://depts.washington.edu/civilr/interviews.htm.
32 Local histories of the Panthers are important. See, for instance, Jones, *The Black Panther Party (Reconsidered);* Yohuru Williams and Jama Lazerow, eds., *Liberated Territory: Untold Local Perspectives on the Black Panther Party* (Durham: Duke University Press, 2009); Williams, *From the Bullet to the Ballot;* Jakobi Williams, "'Don't No Woman Have to Do Nothing She Don't Want to Do': Gender, Activism, and the Illinois Black Panther Party," *Black Women, Gender & Families,* no. 2 (2012).
33 The future of Black Power Studies might consider the effects of parents' activism in the Black Power Movement on their children. Here I am thinking of the children

who ate at the free breakfast programs hosted by the Panthers, the ones that participated in some of the very first Kwanzaa celebrations, and those that witnessed federal agents and officers harass, abuse, and arrest their parents. Separately and perhaps interrelatedly, we might also consider children activists of the Black Power Movement. I look forward to the work of my colleague Dara Walker who focused on high school student activism in Detroit, as I see this as a step in the right direction. See, for example, Dara Walker, "Black Power and the Detroit High School Organizing Tradition," *AAIHS* (blog), August 16, 2018, https://www.aaihs.org/black-power-and-the-detroit-high-school-organizing-tradition-2/.

34 Interview with Mabel Williams, August 20, 1999. Interview K-0266. Southern Oral History Program Collection (#4007), interview by David Cecelski, Transcript, August 20, 1999, Southern Historical Collection, The Wilson Library, the University of North Carolina at Chapel Hill.

35 Craig S. Pascoe, "The Monroe Rifle Club: Finding Justice in an 'Ungodly and Social Jungle Called Dixie.,'" in *Lethal Imagination: Violence and Brutality in American History,* ed. Michael A. Bellesiles (NYU Press, 1999).

36 Tim Tyson writes, "Finding himself virtually a one-man NAACP chapter, Williams turned first to the African American veterans with whom he had stood against the Klan that night back in 1946." Timothy B Tyson, Randolph Boehm, and Daniel Lewis, *A Guide to the Microfilm Edition of The Black Power Movement. Part 2, Part 2,* (Bethesda, MD: University Publications of America, 2002).

37 *Black Power Movement. Part 3, Papers of the Revolutionary Action Movement* (Bethesda, Md.: University Publications of America, n.d.).

38 Cecelski interview with Mabel Williams; Mabel Williams O.H. 1694, interview by Joan V. Feeney, Tape Recording, August 19, 1978, Black History Collections, Center for Oral and Public History, California State University, Fullerton.

39 For more on his recollections, see Wanda Sabir, "Growing Up Revolutionary: An Interview with John Williams, Son of Mabel and Robert F. Williams," *San Francisco Bay View* 3, no. 8 (n.d.): 06.

40 Pero Gaglo Dagbovie, "'God Has Spared Me to Tell My Story: Mabel Robinson Williams and the Civil Rights-Black Power Movement,'" *The Black Scholar* 43, no. 1–2 (2013): 69–88.

41 One might also consider the ways that Black Power is being portrayed in films and TV. My hope is that greater access to resources will result in accurate depictions of Black Power activists and the movement they built.

42 Scholars have interviewed Abiodun for their projects, but these interviews are not available to the public. For example, see Teishan A. Latner, *Cuban Revolution in America: Havana and the Making of a United States Left, 1968–1992* (UNC Press, 2018).

43 Scholarship at the intersections of the Black Power Movement, medicine, health, and health care is necessary. For example, see Eana Meng, "Reflections on (Re)Making History: African American Acupuncturists and the Archives of Tolbert Small," *Asian Medicine* 16, no. 2 (October 29, 2021): 295–309, https://doi.org/10.1163/15734218-12341495; Alondra Nelson, *Body and Soul: The Black Panther Party and the*

Fight against Medical Discrimination (Minneapolis: University of Minnesota Press, 2011).

44 In 2007 eight former Black Panthers were arrested for allegedly murdering Sgt. John Young in San Francisco in 1971. The "San Francisco 8" case included Herman Bell, Jalil Muntaqim, Richard Brown, Richard O'Neal, Ray Boudreaux, Hank Jones, Francisco Torres, and Harold Taylor. The evidence for the case was based on statements made by three of the men after police in New Orleans tortured them for several days employing electric shock, cattle prods, beatings, sensory deprivation, plastic bags, and hot, wet blankets for asphyxiation. In 1975 a California judge threw out the case after finding the involuntary statements coerced. In 2007, with no new evidence, the government attempted again to try the men for the murder. After a long and hard battle, charges were dropped against most of the men. Muntaqim and Bell were already incarcerated at the time of the retrial. Bell pleaded guilty to voluntary manslaughter in the death of Young. Muntaquim pleaded no contest to conspiracy to commit voluntary manslaughter.

45 I want to highlight the efforts in this Digital Humanities Project "Black Power in Washington D.C.," accessed June 3, 2022, https://experience.arcgis.com/experience/5e17e7d1c4a8406b9eaf26a4eae77103/page/Home/.

46 I made a similar observation of Stephan Bradley's brilliantly written and researched book on the student movement at Columbia. See Jasmin Young, "Stephan Bradley: Harlem vs. Columbia University Black Student Power," *Journal of African American Studies* 16 (March 4, 2011): 168–70.

5

"Everybody's Born for Something"

An Oral History Interview with Mabel Williams

In the following transcription, which is an excerpt from a longer oral history interview, Black Power activist Mabel Williams speaks with historian David Cecelski about the lifelong freedom struggles she, her husband Robert, and their family waged against white supremacy. This interview was conducted by Cecelski in 1999, as part of the Southern Oral History Program's "Listening for a Change" project at the University of North Carolina. As fellow natives of North Carolina, the conversation opens around a discussion of how the Williams's activism might be remembered in the town of Monroe and the Tar Heel State more broadly North Carolina. It then covers significant ground through Mabel Williams's (once-forgotten) role in the Monroe NAACP as well as sweeping, lyrical reflections her family's legacies in the Black Power Movement.

NOTE: Page numbers listed indicate the section of the original transcript excerpted here.

David Cecelski [hereafter "DC"]: There'd be a little statue of Robert and you up at the courthouse and probably in the museum at the center for tolerance and struggle. I see a lot of signs about Williams Memorial.

Mabel Williams [hereafter "MW"]: Well, we—. It doesn't have to be—it really doesn't have to be a Robert Williams Memorial. It doesn't have to be but the seeds that he planted in my mind, in my family's mind, in a lot of people. I think those seeds have to be nourished and hopefully, eventually, there will be some young white Monrovians who will catch that seed, nurture that seed and let it grow in Monroe. And then we can feel—I can feel better about Monroe. I haven't seen that yet. And I really hope and pray that it will come in my lifetime.

***

MW: Yeah. I think it affected the black community all over because at last it made them see that, "Well, no, we don't need to accept this lying down and doing nothing. We need to stand up and when we stand up and say, 'no,' we have a greater impact." If we look at—. This is a story that Robert liked to tell all the time. You go by a school and it's a Martin Luther King school. And a little black child says to his mother, "Mama, who is a Martin Luther King?" The mother replies, "Martin Luther King was a civil rights man. He was a great leader of the black people. He loved his people. And he led them in a non-violent fight, struggle. And as a result of that now we have integration [END Page 21] and blah, blah, we." And he said, "Well, oh, what happened to Martin Luther King?" "Well, he was killed." "Why was he killed?" "He was killed because he loved his people and struggled for his people" etceteras, etceteras, etceteras. Okay. Go down the road and here's a Medgar Evers University. Same scenario. "Well, mama who was Medgar Evers?" And she explains who Medgar Evers was. "Well, what happened to him?" "He was killed because he struggled for his people. He loved his people. And the racists killed him. They killed him." Malcolm X. "Well, mama this is Malcolm X Boulevard. Who is Malcolm X?" Same story. "He loved his people. He struggled for his people. And he was killed." And the message that that is giving to young people, young black people, is if you love your people and you struggle to raise their level you will be killed. So what young person is going to want to become a Malcolm X, a Martin Luther King or Medgar Evers or any of those martyrs that—. Now we've got Martin Luther King holiday, you know.

***

MW: Who's going to want to pattern themselves after those people? Not anybody. No—And now you look out there. Who's leading? Who's leading, you know. What kind of leadership do you have? Who wants to step in those footsteps? Nobody. But then you've got a Robert F. Williams who—as he liked to say, "Went home to Mt. Vernon" [Laughter] "and lived out his days as a gentleman." Well, like the president went home to Mt. Vernon and lived out his days as a gentleman.

DC: Surrounded by his family.

MW: Yes. Surrounded by his family and loved ones, and so forth and so on [END Page 22].

DC: Had a long life.

MW: Had a long life, long fruitful life. Loved his people, struggled for people, fought for his people not only nationally, not only in North Carolina. Not only in Monroe, let's say, not only in North Carolina. Not only in the United States, but all over the world. Went all over the world and continued to struggle for his people and then went home to become a gentleman farmer, you know. So hey, maybe, maybe this is the kind—. That's the kind of example that should be out there in front of, not only black children, but white children as well. Hey, if you take the side of the people and you struggle for the best interests of the people—

DC: The side of good.

MW: And the side of good. And hook yourself to that star. Then your life is worthwhile. And that's the legacy that I would like to see for the Robert F. Williams' story. That's the legacy that I'd like to see.

DC: And it goes beyond, I mean, you're right. It goes way beyond like the gun thing.

MW: Yes, way beyond that.

DC: Because it's a—. That, I mean, guns to capture a young person's imagination.

MW: Yes, yes, yes.

DC: In a way that having a milkshake poured in your head at a lunch counter does not.

MW: Right. Of course [END Page 23].

DC: But it's something else, don't you think when a child hears about Robert standing up for himself in this way or any of the other people that you think of [unclear] who are [unclear] the—. You know people like George Washington—. It's [unclear]. It's not necessarily just that—. It's not that they're—. That they're willing to use violence.

MW: Yes.

DC: But one sees something more behind that. And what do you think someone's going to see? What was behind the shotgun? What kind of—what would be good to see in Robert?

MW: I think they would see a person who really knows that one person can make a difference. One person standing up can definitely make a difference. In not only his life but in the lives of other people. And that that one person—. Rob believed that we all had that responsibility. That everybody's born for something. Everybody is here for a purpose.

And that we—. Some people live their lives and they just eat, and sleep and die and never do anything. They don't have any causes. They don't have any purpose. And they think that there is no purpose. Maybe the purpose is just to get money, have a good time, play.

DC: They certainly don't have anything that they're willing to die for.

MW: Nothing that they're willing to die for. But you should have something that you're willing to die for that gives you a reason to live.

DC: That's a nice way to put it [END Page 24].

MW: And I think that that was the legacy, one of the legacies that he left. And I remember one newspaper article during the time that Robert had said about self-defense. One newspaper article came out and said that he was advocating the indiscriminate killing of white babies in their cribs. Now you know that was horrible. Making people think that this man—. Here's a crazy man out here who is trying to get all the white folks killed. That was just to mobilize white folks against him. And against what was going on that was really the right thing in the society to be happening at the time. So—

DC: Where did he get that kind of—?

MW: I think it was passed down through his grandmother, his grandfather and all the way down from slavery. His grandmother came out of slavery literate, knowing how to read and write. Having been the offspring of a white slave master and a black slave. His grandfather came out of slavery knowing how to read and write. And determined to teach their children that they were as good as anybody on this earth. And that they should stand up for what was right and good. And I think that's another thing that the white South, and white Monroe especially, has not lived up to. I remember I was talking to Robert's brother right before I came here. He still lives in Detroit and he's eight years old. And he remembers going into Sechrest Drug Store in Monroe, and one of the clerks coming up to his daddy. He was a little boy with his daddy. And the clerk came up to his daddy and said, "John you know we're cousins." This white clerk said to Robert's father, "John, you know we're cousins. But don't tell [END Page 25] anybody," you know. So my eighty-year old brother-in-law remembers that to this day. But those family members, family members would never accept the fact that—like I said—we're all one family even though we're black and white.

DC: They don't want to treat people like family.

MW: They don't want to treat people like family. And they refuse to acknowledge the fact that they're family because we're so different because we have that one bit of black blood, you know, that makes us black.

DC: Right. So you think—. Robert had this way back and his grandmother, I understand, was his special—

MW: Oh yeah, was his special person that he loved and taught him about world events and got him interested in reading newspapers early on. And, yeah, she was a very—. And handed him a rifle that his grandfather had used way back, and a musket-loaded rifle, which I still have.

DC: Do you?

MW: Yes, yes.

DC: That's [unclear].

MW: Yes. So his brother also told me that his grandmother looked white. And he said one day a white insurance man came by and said to his grandmother, "Are you the only white family in this nigger neighborhood?" And said she looked at him and said, "Don't you ever say that to me again. I am not white. I am black. And this is not a nigger neighborhood. This is a black neighborhood." [Laughter]

DC: Good for her. Lucky he didn't get shot [END Page 26].

MW: Yes. He's lucky he didn't get shot. I remember reading some report when one of Robert's aunts was visited by the FBI. And he wrote that she was more—she was worse than Robert after Robert had left Monroe. She said, "Well this is a no-good town." And she should've burned the damn town down. That was one of the direct descendants of this grandmother, her daughter, who made that—. Aunt Cora. She was really a wonderful person, too. But, yeah, he got—. He had a tradition of struggle and of anger at the society for refusing to recognize people as people. And I think that's—. Robert didn't like to talk about it. His older brother John would talk about it. But Robert didn't like to talk about that connection. So he wouldn't talk about it very much. But his older brother would.

DC: I wonder why not? [unclear]

MW: I told him that he wanted to deny that portion of his—that German stubborn portion of his heritage. And he would only claim the black portion [Laughter] because they denied him. I think that's the reason why. And he didn't like that part of it. But, you know, that's a reality that we face. That is a reality when you start to go back and research and find—. I don't remember which president said it was the most inhumane form of slavery he'd ever seen because people were selling their own sons and daughters into slavery. And the South knew that they were doing that. They knew that they—. They knew and they have never faced up to that fact. They have never faced up. Monroe has never faced up to the fact.

DC: Everybody [unclear]. You have to have a humane society because we're all kin

[END Page 27].

MW: Yes.

DC: And, of course, how we treat our kin as well. I mean that's—. You're not southern if you don't, I mean, [unclear].

MW: Yeah, yeah. I—one of the presidents now, one of the old presidents they have found that—

DC: Jefferson.

MW: It's Jefferson that has these two descendants that they did the DNA and found out. Oh yeah. But they said they still won't allow them to be a part of the home place. They can come to the reunion but they still—. So it's not just a Monroe thing.

DC: Apparently they're starting to look at Washington now.

MW: Yes.

DC: Now they can do this DNA thing to answer questions about George Washington as well.

MW: Yes, yes, yes. So. [Laughter]

DC: No surprise.

MW: No surprise, no surprise. So—but that does not negate the fact that there still has to be ongoing struggle. There still has to be ongoing struggle in order to overcome all of the evils of the past. And I think because our capitalist society at this stage is so—. We have so engaged all of our people, black and white and all, into materialism that it is becoming more and more difficult to have any meaningful human struggles, social struggles that tie people together—that tie people together. And it gets back to those people who have [END Page 28] opted for the good teaching their own—their young people that we have something beyond stuff and things. There's something important in this world that is more important than gathering toys and stuff and things. And there's a human element out here that we need to be concerned with. And I'm hopeful that that is going to happen. I'm hopeful that that is going to happen.

DC: [unclear]

MW: Yes, yes, yes. But I'm—

DC: [unclear] Monroe and I can see you wouldn't have got where you are without [unclear] that you seem to have. [unclear] exactly what's in front of your eyes [unclear] further vision or something.

MW: Yes. And one of the things for me personally is that I think this whole experience of my life has taught me that where we are in the world today there is no set solution out there. That the—there's no ism that's going to do it. It is not coming out of any political, specific political force that's out there right now. It's something that's going to come out of something that we don't even have control over. But we know that once we identify with it that it's going to come. And I think it has to do with spiritual. We're in kind of a spiritual warfare. And I think that that's where the solution is coming from. I'm wondering if our country, our beloved country, this time is on the edge of the Roman— where the Roman Empire was before it went plummeting down. A lot of people don't like to think about that, you know. But everything lives—everything born lives and dies, right? And we would be blind if we didn't know that societies do the same thing [END Page 29]. But then we have to have a belief and a hope that a society will be developed that can be better. We haven't seen the best of what this society has to offer this world. I hope not. I'm sure, I'm sure not. We haven't seen the best.

DC: [unclear] you feel like with especially the end of the Cold War and everything, all of a sudden [unclear], you know, it's like, okay, we're here. And all of a sudden everyone's starting to look inward like you said. Most at a national level. It's like well, all those years [unclear] was to beat the Soviets. And now they have this huge empire [unclear].

MW: Right.

DC: And we're looking [unclear].

MW: Not much there. All they're doing is grasping and grasping and grasping.

***

MW: And people have to, like I said, they have to make a choice, you know. Do they want to be a part of the mean-spirited evil forces that are going on? Or do they want to be a part of the solution, you know. It's like the civil rights song, "What Side Are You On?" Hey, come on.

Source: Mabel Williams, Interview by David Cecelski, August 20, 1999, Interview K-0266. Southern Oral History Program Collection (#4007), Southern Historical Collection, University of North Carolina at Chapel Hill.

6

"Mr. Muhammad Says All of This Is Possible for You and Me"

Elijah Muhammad, *Muhammad Speaks,* and Black Nationalism during the Space Age

D'WESTON HAYWOOD

By the early 1960s, Elijah Muhammad, the leader of the Nation of Islam (NOI), was certain he could provide Black people a liberation far greater than civil rights, even greater than a Black Nationalism in pursuit of separate territory in the US. Against protracted civil rights struggles and intransigent racial oppression, Muhammad intended to claim the planet earth for Black people with the aid of a divine spaceship designed to destroy white power in the known world. Many scholars have analyzed the NOI's ideologies and demands for a separate Black territory, but have overlooked this other, critical side of Muhammad's Black Nationalism, separatism, and racial ideologies.[1] For Muhammad, Black people's fights for civil rights were inherently limited, however much the movement might change state policies and American society. The movement was fundamentally limited, he thought, because the Black freedom struggle sought inclusion in a bound, terrestrial world that by its very nature and temporality proscribed Black people in accessing their full power. This power lay beyond the natural world on an exclusively Black planet that would be brought about with the help of the "Mother Plane," a forthcoming spaceship.[2] What might at first appear to be merely metaphorical, or even preposterous, actually revealed Muhammad's evolving religious theology and political and racial ideologies, which came to be deeply shaped by the politics of the Space Age and Cold War. Indeed, Muhammad was among the first Afrofuturists, working to expand Black politics by articulating visions of Black liberation located in another space and time.[3] And the NOI's official news organ, *Muhammad*

Speaks, gave vivid form to these radical ideas as Muhammad's writings in and outside the paper explained in even greater detail. In fact, in Black people's long-standing literal and figurative search for alternative spaces where they could achieve complete freedom, Muhammad offered what he called, the "New World," along with the divine technology that would engender it. He believed this New World would ultimately herald real Black Power for Black people on their own Black planet.

Yet, examining these sides of Muhammad's dynamic political and racial imaginary requires historians to attend to the "surreal" dimensions of the Black radical imagination, as historian Robin D. G. Kelley has argued, or to what theorist Paul Gilroy calls a "crossroads," the "special location where unforeseen, magical things happen."[4]

Muhammad's complete rethinking of Black liberation to meet the Space Age and Cold War began in the midst of the Great Depression. Muhammad was born Elijah Poole in 1897 in Sandersville, Georgia. A manual laborer mired in financial struggles, Poole, his wife, and then four children set their sights on Detroit by the 1920s, and like many other black southerners, became swept up in the Great Migration. Poole landed some work in manufacturing plants, though he continued to face financial hardships. But in 1931, he encountered a charismatic itinerant preacher, Wallace D. Fard.[5] Fard preached a complex syncretic theology, mixing Christianity and Islam, Marcus Garvey's Black Nationalism, racial uplift ideology, and Black mysticism preached by the likes of Noble Drew Ali.[6] Fard maintained that he was from Mecca, a descendant of the same tribe as the Prophet Muhammad, who had come to the US to rescue Black people. A 1938 sociological study on the group offers a rare window into the organization's inchoate teachings. Fard called the group the Nation of Islam, among many names, and taught followers that Black people constituted the lost tribe of Shabazz, the "original people, the noblest of the nations of the earth." The author of the study argued that the NOI emerged from "a chain of movements arising out of the growing disillusionment and race consciousness of recent Negro migrants to northern industrial cities." Members claimed to gain from the group a "new conception of themselves," along with a new conception of the world. One member shared, for example, that he had always been a Baptist until he heard a "sermon from the prophet [Fard]," declaring that the "sun stands still," as "the earth we are on was doing all the moving." "That changed everything for me," he asserted, "I was turned around completely."[7]

Muhammad experienced a similar personal and intellectual transformation. In fact, the sociological study mentioned him by name as he became one of Fard's most dedicated disciples. Fard changed Poole's surname to "Karriem" and finally to "Muhammad," and eventually hand-picked Muhammad to be his chief minister. But Fard left Detroit in mid-1934 (NOI theology holds that he disappeared), and infighting ensued. Threats of violence from factions claiming to be Fard's rightful successors prompted Muhammad to move to Chicago in September 1934. Muhammad reestablished the NOI there, a point that the sociological study highlighted, identifying him as the steward of the next iteration of Fard's movement.[8]

And by the 1940s and 1950s, the FBI made careful note of these developments. Muhammad barred members from voting and political participation, including registering for the armed forces. Consequently, many members, including Muhammad himself, were imprisoned for violating the Selective Service Act during World War II and the Korean War.[9] For these reasons, among others, the FBI believed the NOI required close surveillance. Placing informants inside the Nation, their surveillance began as early as the 1940s and crested in the 1960s.[10] Read against the grain, their reports have provided scholars some of the few sketches of the often inscrutable NOI, especially in its formative years before its thought and activities became widely known in the 1960s. To be sure, the FBI marked the NOI a "fanatic negro organization," which, they believed, had no qualms about using violence to facilitate the "overthrow of our constitutional government."[11] Some of the NOI's fiery publications proved this, they reasoned, pointing to the *Final Call*, one of the NOI's early papers. Reportedly, the *Final Call* stated that "of all the governments of the world there never existed one so wicked as America . . . Allah, has stretched forth his hand against the wicked America to bring her down."[12] Shaped by the Cold War, the NOI's rhetoric concerned the FBI, making authorities suspicious of connections between the religious group and Communist Russia.[13] This was not the case. But the NOI's actual rhetorical support of Japanese military aggression and Nationalism during World War II, and their refusal to serve in the armed forces, bolstered this view.[14] Yet, by the late 1950s, Muhammad and the NOI became more invested in following certain discourses around American Nationalism and American popular culture than the FBI cared to recognize.

Indeed, the emergence of the Space Age and the attending Nuclear Age in the 1950s, heralded a watershed in Muhammad's theology and political thought. The post-war world divided into two diametrically opposed spheres of influence, pitting the US and Russia against one another in a duel of ideologies, economies, and military strength that stretched across the globe. And state mobilizations of science and technology came to lay at the center. But the growing drive for greater scientific and technological power in the name of national defense pointed up troubling existential questions about global peace and security, human annihilation, the balance of nature, and the power of 'man' versus the power of God. These questions played out in schools, film, literature, and television, as well as the halls of government. Suburban families built bomb shelters as children practiced "Duck and Cover" drills at school in the case of nuclear attack. Science fiction dominated silver screens with blockbuster Hollywood films, such as *The Day the Earth Stood Still* (1951), *The Beast from 20,000 Fathoms* (1953), *Them!* (1954), and *Attack of the Crab Monsters* (1957). These films popularized aliens, robots, sentient machines, natural disasters, and warnings about nuclear power.[15] President Eisenhower and his administration pursued a cautious yet determined approach to researching space exploration. But science fiction turned real with the 1957 launch of the Soviet satellite, Sputnik, elevating concerns that the Communists had now outstripped the US in scientific advancements and made America vulnerable to attack from the skies. The "Space Race" exploded and the Cold War intensified. Policy experts and the public called for Eisenhower to respond, leading to the creation of the National Aeronautics and Space Administration (NASA) in 1958. NASA and other federal programs were charged with numerous initiatives, not the least of which involved putting an American in space.[16]

In this polarized milieu of science and American Nationalism, international crisis, and power in and beyond the globe, Muhammad became profoundly influenced by these discourses as they provided him new ways to formulate and articulate the NOI's vision of Black liberation. Fard had awakened him to deep spiritual, social, and racial reconsiderations in the 1930s. The Space Age helped Muhammad undergo another shift along these lines. The FBI's report in 1955 shared that the Nation conducted classes on astronomy and mathematics for members, and sometimes called themselves the "moon people."[17] The FBI added that "for years the Cult has taken particular delight in teaching that a 'mother plane' is continually circling the continent of North America," "threatening destruction of the Planet Earth." "There are brilliant black men on this plane from the ages of 12 to 25. It is made of the strongest materials in the world and cannot be bombed by any devil because it flies 600 feet above the distance any plane has climbed." "It has the capacity," the report continued, "of throwing thirty bombs to earth . . . When each bomb comes to a stop it releases a highly poisonous gas . . . after this Allah will come and set the world on fire."[18]

To be sure, the NOI had indeed preached about the "Mother Plane" for years, but this description in 1955 reflected something new that paralleled the political and cultural context of Muhammad's current moment in the Space Age, compared to earlier articulations. For example, in the 1940s, the "Mother Plane" resembled discourses surrounding World War II, as well as the NOI's then pro-Japanese sympathies. "Japan has had for many years a monster airplane known to the Moslems as a 'mother airplane,'" an FBI report shared, "said to carry 1,000 small airplanes, each of which carries bombs, which will be used against the white man . . . The Moslems have also told their people that the Japanese have superior equipment of every kind and description."[19] In this version, Japan seemed to possess the "Mother Plane." Muhammad affirmed that the concept of the "Mother Plane" originated with Fard, which may have indeed been the case, given the NOI's esoteric theology before non-initiates.[20] But the influence of the Space Age on Muhammad's intellectual and political thought continued to bear out in dispensations that grew only more colorful and reflective of this particular political and cultural moment.

Muhammad's 1957 book, *The Supreme Wisdom*, especially revealed this. "Allah has warned us of how He would (one day) destroy the world with bombs, poison gas, and finally fire that would consume and destroy everything of the present world. Not anything of it (the present world of white mankind) would be left," Muhammad wrote. "Allah (has) pointed out to us a dreadful looking plane in the sky that is made like a wheel . . . Ezekiel saw it a long time ago. It was built for the purpose of destroying the present world." Here, the "Mother Plane," which the NOI also called the "Wheel of Ezekiel" or "Ezekiel's Wheel," based on Muhammad's biblical interpretations, changed shape now from its articulation in the 1940s and early 1950s to a more circular form akin to a flying saucer. But rather than serving to transport Black people away from earth in a mass exodus that would hearken to Black people's histories of migration and desires for unencumbered mobility, the "Mother Plane" instead instantiated Black people's claims on a certain fixity, on staying put to seize control of space and place, both within and without Earth. Indeed, from the embers of God's wrath, a "New World (of Truth, Freedom, Justice and Equality) will be built by the so-called Negroes." This "New World" would be a place where "We CAN and WILL live without the white race to rule us, as we did for millions of years before [their] appearance on our planet."[21]

The Cold War excited Muhammad, though in problematic terms, to be sure, in part because the era's embrace of Nationalism and racist thinking helped sanction his own. Muhammad was also inspired by public debates that the Space Age and Nuclear Age might lead to the demise of "civilization" either through an overreliance on technology that displaced human labor or, in the worst-case scenario, through Mutually Assured Destruction (MAD).[22] MAD shaped much of US foreign policy and Cold War engagement strategies, holding that nuclear war would result in the total annihilation of both parties. As civil rights activists used the Cold War to challenge the country to live up to its global image as the beacon of democracy, Muhammad used the Cold War to signal the "War of Armageddon," as he put it. This was a global conflagration that only God's chosen people—Black people—would survive, thereby eliminating white people entirely, he believed.[23] As nationalisms tend to go, here were Muhammad's genocidal desires.[24] In the absence of white people, Muhammad reasoned that the planet would return to its rightful owners in a world-historical repossession of property. Turning the racial implications of contemporary science and science fiction discourses on their head, Muhammad constructed white people into an alien race. "This is OUR earth!," and "no one is going to leave this planet to live on another . . . you can't reach the moon and live on it."[25]

The *Supreme Wisdom* rebuked American power, popular culture, white supremacy, and untapped Black potential, dire messages that exploded before a wider audience in the summer of 1959. Beginning in July, the NOI became the subject of a televised documentary series, entitled, "The Hate that Hate Produced." Journalist, Mike Wallace, opened the program with pointed alarm: "a group of negro dissenters are taking to street corner step ladders, church pulpits, sports arenas, and ballroom platforms across the United States to preach a gospel of hate that would set off a federal investigation if it were preached by southern whites."[26] Unbeknownst to Wallace, that investigation was long-standing. As a slew of politicians and civil rights leaders, as well as major news media, including *Time* and the *New York Times*, denounced the Nation, the FBI composed another report in October 1960. Acknowledging that "within the last year, considerable publicity has been afforded the Nation of Islam," they intended to ascertain the extent of the Nation's membership numbers and influence now, while noting some theological tenets that were new to them. "Originally all people on the Earth were black; however, a man named Yakub took some brown people to an island by a process of selective breeding, which took hundreds of years, produced a man who had white skin, but who was weaker than the black man."[27] "Yakub" (sometimes spelled Yacob in NOI theology) was an evil scientist that created white people, the NOI argued, in different kinds of botched science and eugenic experiments. Religious scholar, Michael Muhammad Knight has pointed out that Wallace D. Fard and/or Muhammad could have pulled and modified the idea of Yakub from a 1913 book about racial origins, *Man: Whence, How and Whither: A Record of Clairvoyant Investigation*. By contrast though, the FBI's 1955 report shared that John the Baptist, not Yakub, was the person responsible for creating the white race also through a centuries-long bungled process of selective breeding.[28] Furthermore, Muhammad's *Supreme Wisdom* argued that white people were first created "using a special birth control method."[29] These discrepancies reflect changing historical developments and technologies, the NOI's evolving ideologies, and, as the FBI admitted in their 1955 and 1960 reports, how interpretive and imaginative NOI leaders and ministers could be.[30] This also reflected Muhammad's determination to counter racial pseudo-science that had shaped much of the twentieth century with some of his own.[31] Outside of their surveillance and reports, however, the FBI fed propaganda to several newspapers across the country so that news outlets could help discredit the NOI.[32] Still, "the white man's press, radio, television, and other media, thrust the Muslims into international prominence," Malcolm X reflected.[33] Indeed, confronting a cascade of controversy, the NOI launched *Muhammad Speaks*.

Founded in May 1960, the Nation's official paper became the chief space, though a discursive one, in which Muhammad, ministers, and rank-and-file members projected the contours of a Black planet soon to come. The 1960 FBI report found that in the summer of 1958, the NOI had initiated a new approach in their publicity and recruiting methods, shifting from proselytizing in order to now "'de-emphasize' the religious aspects of his teachings and to stress the economic benefits to be derived by those Negroes who joined the NOI." For the FBI, Muhammad's newly proposed "Economic Blue Print for the Black Man" indicated this change.[34] This, however, was a misreading. For Muhammad, eschatology and economics were inextricably linked. Elevating economics emphasized preparing Black people for the forthcoming "New World" so that they could unlock their full power. "His goals, aims, and program are plainly outlined in the newspaper," *Muhammad Speaks* declared, as headlines blared: "Some of This Earth for Our Own or Else!," "We Are a Nation In A Nation," "A House Doomed to Fail!," "Black Man is Not Safe in Civilized U. S."[35] And what followed the headlines was no less provocative as the paper printed parts of Muhammad's talks to members, public speeches, and radio addresses virtually verbatim. "You may say [white people] are too powerful, they are going up in heaven on the moon and they are shooting for Venus and other planets," but "the white man's world today is going off scene. Their power is being destroyed by the Divine Will of Almighty God."[36] Black people's "inventive genius," "rich talents," and "brawn" had all been "wasted" in "building and contributing to the greatness of America." But because the white world's destruction was immanent, "the time is long past for the black man to start doing some serious thinking about what he must do to become wholly free."[37] Articles by writers for the paper and individual members only shored up these points. Nation-produced music did too. Advertisements in *Muhammad Speaks* included promotions for Louis X's (later Louis Farrakhan) recorded song reconfiguring earth and space, entitled, "White Man's Heaven Is A Black Man's Hell."[38]

Rank-and-file members and the Fruit of Islam (FOI), the Nation's elite cadre of male members, pushed the publication on street corners and door to door.[39] The paper advised readers that their subscription represented "more than buying a paper . . . It is the building of a hospital . . . It is building a library with more than 25,000 books . . . It is building a school with classroom facilities to prepare students to be Engineers, scientists and doctors from a world of today for tomorrow."[40] The paper's circulation mushroomed over the decade, boasting as many as 500,000 copies per week, becoming the NOI's most lucrative business and its leading entrée to the Nation's ideas.[41] Historian Michael A. Gomez has noted that the NOI's membership numbers ranged from as low as 20,000 to as high as 250,000. The number of sympathizers influenced by *Muhammad Speaks*, for instance, was much harder to estimate.[42]

And it was inside the columns of *Muhammad Speaks* that Muhammad's Black planet took shape. "Elijah Muhammad has proven himself a real leader in bringing a new vision and concept to his people," the paper affirmed.[43] By the mid-1960s, the paper illustrated his blueprints—vivid images of imagined Black-built environments, projections intended to help readers visualize the future earth.[44] Plush farms, ship-building industries, state-of-the-art manufacturing plants and railway systems, fleets of planes, high-tech cities, and smiling Black (male) faces, outlined the infrastructures and landscape of a Black utopia.[45] These fantastical images were drawn by Nation members, such as Gerald 2X and Eugene Majied.[46] That NOI members had established many small businesses, including restaurants, bakeries, clothiers, and barber shops in many urban centers across the country, exemplified the seeds of what was to come. An "Infinite Future Has Now Dawned on the Blackman," a "new world now that must be built," *Muhammad Speaks* charged, "because the old—as we have known this world to be—must be removed to give place for a new world."[47]

The Space Age was helping prove to many Americans, including Muhammad, that the impossible *was* possible, and *Muhammad Speaks* reflected this. Even still, the paper also argued that the Space Age helped prove other things, particularly that the structures of white power were not at all interested in investing state resources in Black freedom. Here, Muhammad joined other Black leaders in criticizing the large sums of federal dollars being spent on space exploration over ameliorating impoverished conditions in Black communities.[48] "All of this grief you and I must suffer; all of these burdens we must bear," Muhammad stated, "it is beyond comprehension that the American government—Mistress of the Seas, Lord of the Air, Conqueror of Outer Space, Squire of the Land and Prowler of the Deep Bottoms of the Oceans—is unable to defend us from assault and murder on the streets."[49] Muhammad's demand for land to establish a separate Black nation remained a key feature of the NOI's Black Nationalism, to be sure, but in the broader context of the Nation's political imaginary shaped by the Space Age, this goal functioned as a temporary solution. The land was a placeholder in the interim that would enable Black people to remain safe from racial violence and nuclear war in the West as they prepared for the "New World" and God's destruction of the old. "I am not begging for states. It is immaterial to me, if the white government does not want to give us anything . . . I am not going to start a war with them to take land, because all of it belongs to us," Muhammad insisted. "We, the Muslims, are the true owners of the heavens and the earth."[50]

The FBI remained alarmed as the paper circulated Muhammad's radical ideas. "Why is the NOI seemingly more important today than at any time in its history?," a report in May 1965 thundered. "While the majority of Negroes in the United States do not rush to join the NOI," they acknowledged, "many seem to respect it. Among those who do not join, few participate in any criticism of it. The Muslim advocacy of black supremacy arouses the sympathy of many Negroes. They silently applaud the boldness of Elijah and his ministers."[51] And this was the case even though they found

Muhammad in one instance, according to the report, "rambling" for "over three hours" in a speech before a crowd of 3000 on topics that "ranged from economics to moon flights, from Islam to short skirts on women, and from the thread of death to men on mars."[52] The "cult newspaper," as they put it, was one crucial source of the NOI's spike in popularity. A "new assertive mood frequently called Black Nationalism,' rising among the Negroes in this country," was another factor, one that was indeed building especially among young Black activists. These were developments that the NOI had certainly helped influence over the last several years.[53] "Generally 24 to 28 pages in length," *Muhammad Speaks* was "superior to the average Negro paper in layout and technical quality," the FBI opined. "Since mid-1964, more and more pictures have been printed in color . . . On the front page of every issue, an article by Elijah Muhammad, usually accompanied by his photograph, dramatically sets forth some phase of his teachings. Very often, also appearing on the front page is either a large picture or a drawing which emphasizes racial strife," the FBI chagrined. "Throughout the paper, nearly everything printed tends to aggravate the soreness of race relations in the United States and around the world . . . Always, the white man is portrayed as the brutal oppressor and the black man as the innocent victim." The FBI observed that "many photographs and pictorial sketches are included throughout each issue of the paper," pointing to some of its fantastical illustrations of Muhammad's "New World."

Importantly, they found that the paper was critical to the NOI's recruitment and public support. *Muhammad Speaks* "is another money-making enterprise. FOI captains regularly emphasize to members that 'the number-one program is selling the newspaper.'" "Readers are thus enticed to clip and mail these coupons," the FBI continued, "indicating thereon that they wish to contribute to the '3-Year Economic Plan,' or desire to subscribe to 'Muhammad Speaks,' or perhaps want to purchase books and other products for sale by NOI shopkeepers."[54]

Some of these "books and other products" included albums of Muhammad's recorded speeches, and, by July 1965, his manifesto, *Message to the Blackman*. Several of the book's chapters drew from articles first published in *Muhammad Speaks*.[55] The book emphasized his doctrine of separation, as well as revealed his fascination with and critique of the Space Age. Indeed, the book showed the extent to which Muhammad's thought had come to not only revolve around land and territory, as many scholars have shown, but just as crucially, the skies. Both represented to him imbricated terrains of race and power. "Whatever is in the heavens and whatever is in the earth submits to the God of black mankind—the sun, the moon, the stars and the powers that uphold them are from the original black nation."[56] "All the mighty men of science and modern warfare have been called in an effort to devise instruments and weapons against God and the armies of heaven," he maintained, "Do you not see that [white people] are trying to make themselves a satellite to make you believe that they are the masters of the heavens and earth."[57]

Along these lines, *Message to the Blackman* warned of apocalyptic "battles" in space. Here, the ultimate struggle for Black freedom would not take place in courts, the halls of Congress, or through marches in the streets of American cities, as civil rights activists had been pressing; nor was it to play out on the terrestrial battlefields that typified Western warfare. Rather, "the final war or battle between God and the devils [is] in the sky." The signs were visible, Muhammad contended, in Cold War jockeying and brinkmanship, raging anti-colonial struggles, and Black people's rising militancy at home. These developments "testify to the truth that something of the greatest magnitude is about to take place." The "great Ezekiel's wheel and the unity of the Muslim world" were coming to destroy the known world and replace it with a Black planet—"a new world of justice and righteousness" for the "inheritors of the earth, the so-called Negroes."[58] Contemporary tabloid reports of sightings of "flying saucers" in different parts of the country, according to *Muhammad Speaks,* provided further proof that the "Mother Plane" was approaching its descent.[59]

When Black Power exploded around 1966, it provided more proof that Muhammad's prophetic vision was materializing, the NOI argued. Writers for the paper claimed that "Black Power Theme Based on the Messenger's Program."[60] The origins of Black Power were more complex than this, to be sure. Its politics and consciousness sprung from young Black activists frustrated with the pace of the Black freedom struggle, the protest strategies deployed by an older civil rights establishment, and the intransigence of racism, urban poverty, police brutality, racial violence, and colonialism, frustrations that all bubbled over into a new Black militancy.[61] But the NOI, especially Malcolm X, indeed influenced these developments, and some Black radicals seemed to agree. A conference in 1967, for example, involving Floyd McKissick of the Congress of Racial Equality (CORE), H. Rap Brown of the Student Nonviolent Coordinating Committee (SNCC), and Ron Karenga of US, among others, showed that "the Messenger's example through the Nation of Islam and program was taking root among Black people."[62] *Muhamad Speaks* reported Stokely Carmichael saying,

"The Honorable Elijah Muhammad has helped more black people in the country. This proves he has real power." And Carmichael said this as he was "holding high Messenger Muhammad's popular book 'Message to the Blackman'" before a crowd.[63] The NOI capitalized on this moment as its visionary forerunner, but argued that Muhammad's concept of Black Power had originated with God.[64] For these reasons, if "someone has the key to 'black power,'" *Muhammad Speaks* editorialized, "without a shadow of doubt, I believe Muhammad is that man."[65]

But as many Black Power advocates called for Black-centered curriculum and educational institutions, revolutionary changes in the politics, economies, and conditions of Black communities, an end to police brutality, redistributions of power in the state, and a revolutionary Black Internationalism, some activists came to think that Muhammad and the NOI's long-term plans for Black freedom fell short of anything radical. Huey P. Newton was one. Newton once attended an NOI mosque in Oakland, California, before co-founding the Black Panther Party for Self-Defense in October 1966. For a time, he admired the Nation's stated platform, enough to model the Panthers' platform, "What We Want, What We Believe," on Muhammad's "What the Muslims Want, What the Muslims Believe," which was regularly printed in *Muhammad Speaks*. But for Newton, the Nation was among many Black groups that were "so dedicated to rhetoric and artistic rituals that they had withdrawn from living in the Twentieth Century. Sometimes their analyses were beautiful, but they had no practical programs."[66] "I did read their paper regularly to follow the speeches and ideas of Malcolm," Newton acknowledged, but "I had had enough of religion . . . References to God or Allah did not satisfy my stubborn questioning."[67]

But what was it to believe in the impossible, given that what many considered impossible appeared to be manifesting under the US and Russia on the world stage, as well as before an observant Muhammad? The idea that Black people should not wage their battles on the ground because they could be won if they only took to the sky where the ultimate tool for Black resistance was waiting, is significant for reconsidering Black Power, in addition to Black Nationalism, Black intellectual and political thought, as well as the historian's craft. As historian Robin D. G. Kelley has suggested, the ways Black people resist, especially those, who are part of the Black working class, are multivalent, and may draw from "spiritual empowerment," not merely as "a potential site for political organizing" but also "the sacred, the spirit world . . . as veritable weapons to protect themselves or to attack others." How should historians "interpret divine intervention," Kelley asks.

What could otherwise be dismissed as a "case of 'false consciousness'" obscures the myriad ways such thinking on the part of Black people carried "real power" for believers and sustained them against racial oppression.[68] As Abdul Basit Naeem, a Pakistani Muslim and columnist for *Muhammad Speaks,* commented, Muhammad's teachings had their "baffling (unorthodox) aspects, but my own inability to grasp them cannot minimize the movement's significance."[69] Indeed, Muhammad continued to elaborate on the "Mother Plane" until his death in 1975. In 1973, for instance, *Muhammad Speaks* published his exegesis of "Ezekiel's Wheel" in a series that ran for several months. The "Mother Plane" remained "the greatest mechanical defender, powered by the spirit of Allah, to protect us, the Black people on the face of the earth." In this dispensation, it maintained the same flying saucer shape it took on in the late 1950s. But unlike previous iterations, it was now "capable of carrying many people in it," perhaps indicating then a new option for Black freedom in an ever-changing racial and political imaginary.[70]

In their 1955 report on the NOI, the FBI remarked that "nothing is more pleasing to them than to indulge in the reverie of wishful thinking." And yet, for all their "wishful thinking," the Bureau remained convinced that the Nation's belief "in the destruction of the devil" and "the coming of Allah to this country" merited rigorous surveillance.[71] In fact, this surveillance intensified under the FBI's infamous Counter Intelligence Program (COINTELPRO). In 1967, the Bureau identified Muhammad and the NOI by name among several integrationist and radical Black organizations, all of which the FBI strung together as "hate-type organizations" despite stark differences in their ideologies, protest strategies, and goals. Through this covert operation, the FBI intended to "expose, disrupt, misdirect, discredit, or otherwise neutralize" the groups, internal memoranda shared. Though the FBI now regarded Muhammad to be "less of a threat because of his age," his ideas about the "approaching 'War of Armageddon'" remained deeply troubling.[72] By 1968, concerns about the Nation only festered. The NOI promoted "hatred of all whites as enemies, a separation of blacks from whites, a black supremacy, the destruction of America," another COINTELPRO memorandum stated, "and occasionally refers to the readiness of NOI spaceships hovering over the planet to carry out the revolution."[73] COINTELPRO struck at the very point that Muhammad had been making: America and its power structures were not invested in Black freedom. For Muhammad, this reality signaled the need for a boldly imagined Black liberation. As America dreamed of the infinite possibilities of science and space exploration, so did Muhammad. But rather than seeing this inspiring political and cultural moment as the apex of American power, Muhammad figured it as the decline of white supremacy, ebbing in time for the dawn of a Black Power not quite of this earth.

Notes

1. See, for example, Michael A. Gomez, *Black Crescent: The Experience and Legacy of African Muslims in the Americas*, (New York: Cambridge University Press, 2005), 276, 295; Jeffrey O. G. Ogbar, *Black Power: Radical Politics and African American Identity*, (Baltimore: Johns Hopkins University Press, 2004); Michael E. Sawyer, *Black Minded: The Political Philosophy of Malcolm X*, (London: Pluto Press, 2020).
2. C. Eric Lincoln, *The Black Muslims in America*, (Grand Rapids, MI: W. B. Eermans, 1994), 21.
3. See, for example, Mark Dery, "Black to the Future: Interviews with Samuel R. Delany, Greg Tate, and Tricia Rose," in Mark Dery, *Flame Wars: the Discourse of CyberCulture*, (Durham: Duke University Press, 1994), 179–222; Francesca T. Royster, "Labelle: Funk, Feminism, and the Politics of Flight or Fight," *American Studies*, 52:4 (2013): 77–98; William Sites, *Sun Ra's Chicago: Afrofuturism and the City*, (Chicago: University of Chicago Press, 2020).
4. Robin D. G. Kelley, *Freedom Dreams: The Black Radical Imagination*, (Boston: Beacon Press, 2002), 4–5; Paul Gilroy, *Small Acts: Thoughts on the Politics of Black Cultures*, (New York: Serpent's Tail, 1993), 193.
5. See also, Ula Yvette Taylor, "Building a Movement, Fighting the Devil," in Ula Yvette Taylor, *The Promise of Patriarchy: Women and the Nation of Islam*, (Chapel Hill: The University of North Carolina Press, 2017), 18–30.
6. Claude Andrew Clegg III, *An Original Man: The Life and Times of Elijah Muhammad*, (New York: St. Martin's Press, 1997), 6, 14–25, 29–40, 116; Susan Nance, "Mystery of the Moorish Science Temple: Southern Blacks and American Alternative Spirituality in 1920s Chicago," *Religion and American Culture: A Journal of Interpretation*, 12:2 (Summer 2002): 123–166; Gomez, *Black Crescent*, 276, 295.
7. Erdmann Doane Beynon, "The Voodoo Cult Among Migrants in Detroit," *American Journal of Sociology*, 43:6 (May 1938): 894–907.
8. Erdmann Doane Beynon, "The Voodoo Cult Among Migrants in Detroit," *American Journal of Sociology*, 43:6 (May 1938): 894–907.
9. See for example, *Chicago Defender*, "Indicts 12 on Sedition," October 24, 1942; *Chicago Defender*, "D. C. Cultist Convicted of Draft Dodge," October 24, 1942; Elijah Muhammad, *Message to the Blackman in America*, (Phoenix: Secretarius MEMPS Publications, 1973) 321. See also, Malcolm X and Alex Haley, *The Autobiography of Malcolm X*, (New York: Ballentine Books, 1992), 334. See also, George Breitman, *By Any Means Necessary: Speeches, Interviews and a Letter by Malcolm X*, (New York: Pathfinder, Inc., 1970), 158.

10 Michael Muhammad Knight, "'I am Sorry, Mr. White Man, These are Secrets You are Not Permitted to Learn': The Supreme Wisdom Lessons and Problem Book," *Correspondences* 7: 1 (2019): 167–200. See also, Garrett Felber, *Those Who Know Don't Say: The Nation of Islam, the Black Freedom Movement, and the Carceral State*, (Chapel Hill: The University of North Carolina Press, 2019).
11 FBI Report, 1955, https://vault.fbi.gov/Nation%20of%20Islam/Nation%20of20Part%201%of203/view, p. ii–iii, accessed March 2, 2021.
12 FBI Report, 1955, https://vault.fbi.gov/Nation%20of%20Islam/Nation%20of20Part%201%of203/view, p. 41, accessed March 2, 2021.
13 FBI Report, 1955, https://vault.fbi.gov/Nation%20of%20Islam/Nation%20of20Part%201%of203/view, p. 44, accessed March 2, 2021. See also, *MS*, "What Is An 'Un-American?,'" December 1961.
14 See also, Ernest Allen Jr., "When Japan was 'Champion of the Darker Races': Satokata Takahashi and the Flowering of Black Messianic Nationalism," *The Black Scholar*, 24:1 (1994): 23–46.
15 Nicholas Michael Sambaluk, *The Other Space Race: Eisenhower and the Quest for Aerospace Security*, (Annapolis, MD: Naval Institute Press, 2015), 40, 63. See also, Jacqueline Foertsch, *Reckoning Day: Race, Place, and the Atom Bomb in Postwar America*, (Nashville: Vanderbilt University Press, 2013).
16 Sambaluk, *The Other Space Race*, 75–92.
17 FBI Report, 1955, https://vault.fbi.gov/Nation%20of%20Islam/Nation%20of20Part%201%of203/view, p. 84, accessed March 2, 2021. See also, Michael Muhammad Knight, "'I am Sorry, Mr. White Man, These are Secrets You are Not Permitted to Learn': The Supreme Wisdom Lessons and Problem Book," *Correspondences* 7: 1 (2019): 167–200.
18 FBI Report, 1955, https://vault.fbi.gov/Nation%20of%20Islam/Nation%20of20Part%201%of203/view, p. 43, accessed March 2, 2021.
19 Ernest Allen Jr., "When Japan was 'Champion of the Darker Races': Satokata Takahashi and the Flowering of Black Messianic Nationalism," *The Black Scholar*, 24:1 (1994): 23–46.
20 Edward E. Curtis, "Science and Technology in Elijah Muhammad's Nation of Islam: Astrophysical Disaster, Genetic Engineering, UFOs, White Apocalypse, and Black Resurrection," *Nova Religio: The Journal of Alternative and Emergent Religions*, 20: 1 (2016): 5–31.
21 Elijah Muhammad, *The Supreme Wisdom*, Vol. II, (Hampton, VA: U.B. & U.S. Communications Systems, 1957), 29, 31, 23.
22 *Muhammad Speaks* (*MS*), "30 Minutes to Armageddon," October-November, 1961; *MS*, "Still Last Hired and First Fired," July 5, 1963.
23 Mary Dudziak, *Cold War Civil Rights: Race and the Image of American Democracy*, (Princeton: Princeton University Press, 2011).
24 See, Benedict Anderson, "Patriotism and Racism," in Anderson, *Imagined Communities, Reflection on the Origin and Spread of Nationalism*, revised edition, (New York: Verso, 2006), 145–158. See also, Foertsch, *Reckoning Day*, 165–166.

25　Muhammad, *The Supreme Wisdom*, 25, 40, 37, 82–83.
26　Mike Wallace and Louis E. Lomax, "The Hate that Hate Produced," https://archive.org/details/PBSTheHateThatHateProduced, accessed February 2, 2021. See also, Malcolm X and Haley, *The Autobiography*, 271; Louis E. Lomax, *The Negro Revolt*, (New York: Harper and Row, 1962), 164, 167, 203.
27　FBI Report, "The Nation of Islam," 1960, https://archive.org/details/FBI-Nation-Of-Islam-Monographs/1960-Nation-Of-Islam/page/n89/mode/2up, p. i–iii, 67.
28　FBI Report, 1955, https://vault.fbi.gov/Nation%20of%20Islam/Nation%20of%20Part%201%20of%203/view, p. 49, accessed March 2, 2021; Michael Muhammad Knight, "'I am Sorry, Mr. White Man, These are Secrets You are Not Permitted to Learn': The Supreme Wisdom Lessons and Problem Book," *Correspondences* 7:1 (2019): 167–200. See also, Benjamin Fagan, *The Black Newspaper and the Chosen Nation*, (Athens: The University of Georgia Press, 2016).
29　Muhammad, *The Supreme Wisdom*, 14.
30　FBI Report, 1955, https://vault.fbi.gov/Nation%20of%20Islam/Nation%20of%20Part%201%20of%203/view, p. ii, accessed March 2, 2021.; FBI Report, "The Nation of Islam," 1960, https://archive.org/details/FBI-Nation-Of-Islam-Monographs/1960-Nation-Of-Islam/page/n75/mode/2up, p. 55, accessed March 3, 2021.
31　See, for example, Elazar Barkan, *The Retreat of Scientific Racism: Changing Concepts of Race in Britain and the United States between the World Wars*, (New York: Cambridge University Press, 1992).
32　Malcolm X and Haley, *The Autobiography*, 279.
33　Malcolm X and Haley, *The Autobiography*, 273.
34　FBI Report, "The Nation of Islam," 1960, https://archive.org/details/FBI-Nation-Of-Islam-Monographs/1960-Nation-Of-Islam/page/n55/mode/2up, p. 37, accessed March 3, 2021; *MS*, "1st Economic Program for Black America," July 3, 1964.
35　*MS*, "Would You Like to be an Expert," April 1962; *MS*, October-November, 1961; *MS*, April 1962; *MS*, November 15, 1962; *MS*, June 1962.
36　*MS*, "Anything By a Slave Boss," December 1961.
37　*MS*, "Wasted Genius of Black Man," December 1961.
38　*MS*, May 1962.
39　Malcolm X Papers (MXP), Muhammad to Malcolm, February 8, 1962, Box 3, Folder 8.; MXP, Memorandum, April 25, 1963; MXP, "Recognize all Laborers," Box 11, Folder 3.
40　*MS*, "Your Subscription," July 31, 1962. See also, Ula Yvette Taylor, "The Appeal of Black Nationalism and the Promise of Prosperity," in Taylor, *The Promise of Patriarchy*, 140–168. See also, Brandon K. Winford, *John Hervey Wheeler, Black Banking, and the Economic Struggle for Civil Rights*, (Lexington: University of Kentucky Press, 2020).
41　Ogbar, *Black Power*, 44.; Bruce Perry, *Malcolm: The Life of a Man Who Changed Black America*, (Barrytown, NY: Station Hill, 1991), 220–221. See also, *MS*, "Reach," December 1961.
42　Gomez, *Black Crescent*, 356. See also, Essien-Udom, *Black Nationalism*, 71–72.
43　*MS*, "Muhammad Sparks U.S. Muslim Movement," October-November, 1961.

44 Brian Goldstein, "'The Search for New Forms': Black Power and the Making of the Postmodern City," *Journal of American History*, 103:2 (September 2016): 375–399.
45 See, Alex Zamalin, *Black Utopia: The History of an Idea from Black Nationalism to Afrofuturism*, (New York: Columbia University Press, 2019).
46 See, for example, MS, "Muhammad: How to Eat to Live," December 10, 1965; MS, "Muhammad's Mission to the Nation of Islam," January 15, 1965.
47 MS, "Tuskegee Invites Muhammad!," October 22, 1965; See also, MS, "Build New Business, Make New Jobs For Ourselves and For Others," July 15, 1962; MS, "He Knows Islam is 'Right Weapon' in War on Poverty," December 4, 1964. See also, Malcolm X and Haley, *The Autobiography*, 303, 235. See also, Clegg, *An Original Man*, 235–268. MS, "Can We Rely on Ourselves to Build a New World," October 15, 1965.
48 MS, "Why Spend Billions to Put White Man on the Moon," September 13, 1963.
49 MS, "The Messenger Has the Better Plan," February 5, 1965.
50 MS, "Our Time is Near at Hand," March 3, 1964.
51 FBI Report, "Nation of Islam, Cult of the Black Muslims," 1965, https://archive.org/details/FBI-Nation-Of-Islam-Monographs/1965-Nation-Of-Islam/page/n35/mode/2up, p. 4, 12, accessed March 6, 2021.
52 FBI Report, "Nation of Islam, Cult of the Black Muslims," 1965, https://archive.org/details/FBI-Nation-Of-Islam-Monographs/1965-Nation-Of-Islam, p. 4, 12, 48–49, accessed March 6, 2021.
53 FBI Report, "Nation of Islam, Cult of the Black Muslims," 1965, https://archive.org/details/FBI-Nation-Of-Islam-Monographs/1965-Nation-Of-Islam, p. 59, 4, accessed March 6, 2021.
54 FBI Report, "Nation of Islam, Cult of the Black Muslims," 1965, https://archive.org/details/FBI-Nation-Of-Islam-Monographs/1965-Nation-Of-Islam, 45, 63–66, accessed March 6, 2021.
55 MS, "Send in Your Order Today," July 23, 1965; MS, "Cleveland Opens Massive Sales Drive for Muhammad's 'Message to Blackman,'" December 17, 1965.
56 Muhammad, *Message to the Blackman*, 103–122.
57 Muhammad, *Message to the Blackman*, 268, 109–110.
58 Muhammad, *Message to the Blackman*, 292–293, 268, 270.
59 MS, "Saucer Sightings Recall Messenger's Warnings," April 1, 1966.
60 Muhammad, *Message to the Blackman*, 100, 109, 186–191, 270; MS, "Black Power Theme Based on the Messenger's Program," August 4, 1967.
61 See, for instance, Ogbar, *Black Power*; Peniel E. Joseph, *Waiting Til The Midnight Hour: A Narrative History of Black Power in America*, (New York: Henry Holt and Company, 2006); Hassan Kwame Jeffries, *Bloody Lowndes: Civil Rights and Black Power in Alabama's Black Belt*, (New York: New York University Press, 2009); Donna Jean Murch, *Living for the City: Migration, Education, and the Rise of the Black Panther Party in Oakland, California*, (Chapel Hill: The University of North Carolina, 2010); Martha Biondi, *The Black Revolution on Campus*, (Berkeley: University of California Press, 2014); Rhonda Williams, *Concrete Demands: The Search for Black Power in the 20th Century*, (New York: Routledge, 2015); Robyn C. Spencer, *The Revolution Has Come: Black Power, Gender, and the Black Panther Party in Oakland*,

(Durham: Duke University Press, 2016); Joshua Bloom and Waldo E. Martin Jr., *Black Against Empire: The History and Politics of the Black Panther Party*, (Berkeley: University of California Press, 2016); Ashley D. Farmer, *Remaking Black Power: How Black Women Transformed an Era*, (Chapel Hill: The University of North Carolina Press, 2019).

62 See also, *MS*, "Tells Why Islam Instead of Politics Will Make True Black Power a Reality," August 26, 1966; *MS*, "SNCC Chairman Praises Muhammad," August 12, 1966; *MS*, "See 'Black Power' Growing Influence of Muhammad," August 12, 1966; *MS*, "Impact of Muhammad Reported By Howard Sociologist," November 4, 1966.

63 *MS*, "Carmichael Lauds Role of Last Messenger of Allah," August 19, 1966.

64 *MS*, "Explains Why Mr. Muhammad Alone Holds the Key to True Black Power," August 19, 1966; *MS*, "Messenger Muhammad on Fear of Black Power," January 6, 1967. See also, Clegg, *An Original Man*, 243.

65 *MS*, "Why Radio Won't Contact Messenger on 'Black Power,'" October 28, 1966.

66 Philip S. Foner, ed., *The Black Panthers Speak*, (Cambridge, MA: Da Capo Press, 1970), 273.

67 Huey P. Newton, *Revolutionary Suicide*, (New York: Penguin Books, 2009), 72.

68 Robin D. G. Kelley, *Race Rebels: Culture, Politics, and the Black Working Class*, (New York: Free Press, 1996), 42–43.

69 *MS*, "Muhammad's Message May Baffle Some but It Works," October 15, 1965. See also, Herbert Berg, "Elijah Muhammad: An African American Mufassir?," *Arabica*, 1998, Vol. 45 (4), p. 320–346.

70 *MS*, "O Wheel Mother of Planes," September 7, 1973. See also, for example, *MS*, "Messenger Muhammad's Analysis of Ezekiel's Wheel," August 24, 1973; *MS*, "Inside of Ezekiel's Wheel," September 21, 1973.

71 FBI Report, 1955, https://vault.fbi.gov/Nation%20of%20Islam/Nation%20of20Part%201%20of203/view, p. 46, 48, accessed March 5, 2021.

72 COINTELPRO: Black Extremist, Part 1 of 23, https://vault.fbi.gov/cointel-pro/cointel-pro-black-extremists/cointelpro-black-extremists-part-01-of/view, pgs. 3–4, 69–70, 35, accessed March 15, 2021.

73 COINTELPRO: Black Extremist, Part 1 of 23, https://vault.fbi.gov/cointel-pro/cointel-pro-black-extremists/cointelpro-black-extremists-part-01-of/view, p. 96, accessed March 15, 2021.

7

Excerpt of Elijah Muhammad's Address from *Muhammad Speaks* (1962)

In the following excerpt, Elijah Muhammad speaks of what he sees as the approaching "Judgment" for America. In this speech, he distills much of the theology behind what D'Weston Haywood identifies as "the doctrine of separation" in his essay. Here, he calls upon Black America to recognize and turn away from what he sees as sin and deceit designed by the Devil to bound them for the coming destruction. Although Muhammad does not explicitly discuss ideas about a "Black Planet" as mentioned in the previous essay, the foundation he constructs for such an ideology is more fully detailed here. The enduring legacies of Muhammad's ideas about celestial exploration and Afrofuturism can be seen in the music of hip-hop groups such as Public Enemy, most notably in their 1990 album "Fear of a Black Planet."

Greetings to you, I am Elijah Muhammad, the preacher of freedom, justice, and equality to you, my poor Black people who has been lost in the wilderness of North America for the last 400 or more years. You my dear beloved brothers and sisters that is listening to my voice on this album, I would [hope] that you pay good attention to it. Our subject is the Judgment. Judgment has been taught and we have been warned that it is a day coming that we all will be judged. And whoever Allah have mercy upon, that person will have a great reward bestowed upon him. Because we live in a world guided by the open enemy, the devil himself. Therefore, being lost from our own people, wherein there was no one to teach us, no one to help us, all teachers was prevented from teaching us of our very pitiful condition.

Our fathers fell in when captured by our enemies, the open devil in our native land. Through deceit, here we are today on trial before the God who will judge us all. Who will this God be? The Son of Man, both Bible and Holy Quran declare he will be a man, a son from a man. Son of Man. Not a formly spirit, that the saintly scholars of religion have given this name. To that Judge on that day, the day of Judgment in which we now live, will be a man, for only a man can judge rightly between man and man. Because their nature is alike. Anything other than a man cannot judge our affairs, nor guide us in the right way that we will be successful. It's got to be a man! Thus when is the Day of Resurrection? This is the Day of Resurrection. You're living in it. When is the doom coming? When will be its taking place? Don't hurry for that day because you're living in it now . . .

When will that day come, they keep asking? Maybe you don't have to ask that question—when the judgment will come—it's already here, just go to looking and see what's going on. And then stop and listen: you will bear Elijah's witness that we in it now. Great separation must take place. I have been pleading with you Black brothers and sisters on the last page of our paper, *Muhammad Speaks*, that we should be separated from our heartless enemy, and given someplace— even if it was here—to ourselves. He don't want you to go free for yourself! No. He want to beat and kill you! He want to deceive you! So that you can taste his doom with him yourself. While you have a chance, God has forgiven us before ever that we was born. There somebody's vision of the dry bones of Ezekiel . . . is none other than you. And this lesson teaches you that God did give them life! And they did believe, they bowed to Him and believe. The Holy Quran and Bible both teaches that He will force us to believe since that we are His. We are the people of the righteous. But you has been so foolishly following after evil, now [you have] become lovers of evil and haters of good, like the enemy who is misleading you.

I say my friend, since you are weak as the Holy Quran teaches us the Muslims, if you see something that is going to tempt you, cast your eyes in another direction. How can you love a people and go marry them, take them for husbands and wives—while they have killed your fathers and your people all the day long, ever since they landed on the shores of this country. Why don't you think something like love and respect for yourself and your kind? If they had been treated by you like that, they would not even speak to you only with fire and iron and steel. They would not speak to you. The only thing they want to do is to kill you for mistreating their parents and for chasing their sons and daughters over the land to destroy them. It is awful, my friend . . .

I say my friend, there is none that can stand in this time that we now are in. Suffering the lashes of nature, all nature now has been turned against America to war against her and to destroy her . . . Everything is armed for the destruction of America, her wealth, her money, as the [apostle] James teaches there you around the fourth or fifth chapter. Why is the rich man going to weep and howl for the miseries that is coming upon? You have done injustice to the poor, the so-called American Negro. You have laid up his hand, his wages. You have put them up, buried them in mountains, sent them out of the country to another friend of yours. Storing it up to pay off the enemies of yours when they come against you. They don't accept your pay today, they have wealth. They don't want yours. No way can you pay off your doom. It is set, bound to come to pass. Poor America. As one writer says, "woe to the land that is shattered with wings!" It is America's full of planes, soaring disguise over her country. But woe unto her! The day, the day, the terrible day of the Lord.

She has lived sumptuously. So says the parable of Jesus and the rich man . . . But her labor, her poor old, so-called Negroes, the Black slaves. He suffered for the like of even good food and good clothes and a good shelter. Let them live out of those, burn their homes down if they had a good one, to show you how much he hate you to even to live in a good home. Poison and kill your cattle to keep you from feeding yourself, so that you will be at his mercy. Should not God do something about a people like that? [They] slip around under the cover of darkness and set your house a fire, should not a God of justice do something about this?

This is the Day of Judgment. She will be paid back for all that she has done against you and me. She will be paid back. But she don't believe that she's gonna be paid back! She wants you to think that this is something or these calamities will pass over one day and we will be ruling over you again, Negroes. But this is the way of God in destroying a people in both Bible and Holy Quran . . . Woe to America, the judgment is set and the chastising is going on. The signs that would come to her, prophesized by the prophets of old is now going on. They are here before our eyes . . . That is rain, snow, hail, and earthquakes. Listen for your earthquakes! They are going on in America. Listen to that weatherman tell you what's going on in other states. It's now going on. Listen to your friends tell you over the phone and in their letters what they see, the dreadful things happening. No way out! This has already come to you. The shaking of the earth, the leveling of the cities is the last thing that will happen. And before these things come to pass on America and large-scale, Allah shakes little small places, gives a little small shaking, just to warn 'em! And then at a distance, from afar, she reads what is going on there: trouble, cities is destroyed by earthquakes, rain is wiping away others, storms. I say to you, this is the Judgement. Our wish is to teach you to worry about this Judgment, but this album won't hold it. But I will make another one to finish getting you over into the knowledge that this is the

Judgment and the time have arrived that you and me must take a stand on this side with our God, Allah, and the people of ours, the Black nation, or we will be destroyed with the white nation.

Source: Elijah Muhammad, *Muhammad Speaks: The Judgement of the World is Now!*, Vol. I, (Chicago: Muhammad's Mosques, Vinyl, 1962).

8

"Strength in Your Own Voice"

An Oral History Interview with Nikki Giovanni

In acclaimed poet Nikki Giovanni's 2016 oral history interview with Randi Gil-Sadler, which is excerpted below, she covers a range of topics relating to race and ancestry, her upbringing in Tennessee, American history, Muhammad Ali, and her view of space and Afrofuturism. Gil-Sadler, then a UF PhD student, interviewed Giovanni about her life history and the central ideas and experiences that shaped her writings. The full text of the interview is available through the Samuel Proctor Oral History Program archive. Much like Gwendolyn Zoharah Simmons and Mabel Williams, Giovanni explains how her family relationships, especially with other Black women, shape her views on the world, music, and the craft of cooking. Moreover, Giovanni offers a different view of the need for space exploration than Muhammad. Rather than seeing the Earth as almost irredeemable, she sees the universe beyond as a place for curiosity where Black ingenuity and love can make a difference.

Randi Gil-Sadler [hereafter "RGS"]: Okay, thank you so much for doing this interview, Dr. Giovanni. And I read some of your other interviews, so I want to start off a little bit differently. I want to start with a word association. So I'll say a word and you tell me first thing comes to mind. All right: Tennessee.

Nikki Giovanni [hereafter "NG"]: I was born in Tennessee. I'm a Knoxvillian by birth and as we know Eastern Tennessee was the difference in the Civil War, because Middle Tennessee, Nashville went with the money. And of course Memphis, Western Tennessee, went with the South and if it hadn't been for Knoxville and that area deciding that they were gonna stay with the Union, we would have had a different outcome for the Civil War.

RGS: All right. Next word: poetry.

NG: I write poetry and I enjoy it, and I encourage other people to do it. I try to teach, not poetry, but strength in your own voice. I try to teach my students that what's important is what you know and how you express it.

RGS: Momma.

NG: I have one. [Laughter] My mother passed ten years ago now. I am one. My son is forty-six and I am a grandmother, so I've gone through the whole—.

RGS: All right, Gus.

NG: Gus was my father and he too has passed. He's been, I suppose now, it's seventeen years. I can't pull the math up but Gus was—my mother married him and he was my father, or he is my father; still is.

RGS: Grandmother.

NG: Emma Lou Venia. Had a friend that recently was asking me about that. Emma Lou is my grandmother, and my great-grandmother was Cornelia, and Cornelia Watson was the mother of my grandfather John Brown Watson, who was obviously named John Brown for the revolutionary. And John Brown married Emma Lou and they had three daughters: Yolande Cornelia and Anne-Elizabeth and Agnes Margery, and Agnes is ninety-four years old.

RGS: Wow!

NG: She's still with us—actually she's coming to visit me in two weeks and I have to make some chitlins, I brought the chitlins, I'm going have to clean them and put them on.

RGS: Okay. All right, Muhammad Ali.

NG: Muhammad was a friend. I haven't seen him lately. Both of us are getting old. Ali is maybe two years older than I am, but when the government stripped him of his title—he of course did poetry and Richard Fulton, who did some speaking handling for Ali, asked me, because a lot of people were afraid of getting associated with Ali who was good looking, sweet guy, and he asked me would I do it. Would I read poetry with him, would I travel with him, and I said "Yes." But you know, Ali was a womanizer and his wife was very nervous, but she knew me and she said "Well I don't mind if it's Nikki." But she didn't know, and I don't mind saying that now, is that I never was on the bus. He was on the bus and he would travel to Columbus. He did the bus. I always flew, because I was busy. And so, whoever was on the bus with him was what was going on.

RGS: You didn't know. [Laughter]
NG: Had nothing to do with me. I laughed about that. If I could see him now we would laugh about that.
RGS: Beautiful. Jazz.
NG: I love jazz. My mother was a jazz fan and a good singer, and my sister could play the piano. I don't have any talents like that, but I love jazz and coming down here, I don't have it on now, but I put my ears on every time I'm flying. I put my ears on and I listen I have what are those things?
RGS: iPod?
NG: iPod, and I just listen all the way, fall asleep and wake back up.
RGS: Okay, Black.
NG: I am and it's a term—it'd be very seldom that you would hear me use the term African American. The term that I traditionally use is of course "Black Americans," because we are Americans, and we are Black, and we are the people, and I will speak about that this evening. Black Americans are the people who had to create themselves. So when we came to America, we had to make a decision: "Are we going to be Americans or not?" We are and of course color's gonna come in. If we look at our fellow Americans, we look at German Americans and British Americans. Now we look at Caribbean Americans, and now actually we're looking at Africans who have become here but we didn't have any place to go back to. When we were brought here, in slavery, but nonetheless when we were brought here we knew that we had no place to go so whatever we were gonna be we had to create ourselves here.
RGS: Okay. Two more: Middle Passage.
NG: Middle Passage is the most incredible, incredible historical situation as you know and that is something that I talk about a lot because the fact that we could come from enslavement to what was going to be, as it was at that point, America and come with a sanity, learn a language, create a food, create a music, create a people. Where would we be without Black Americans, it's incredible, and middle passage is what I've been working with NASA. And I'm so excited about that because I really really want NASA to send more Black people into space, and I want Black youngsters, not just—and I like scientists it's not that, but we need the creative people to go into space and we need to put the energy into getting the kids just to go up to the space station and come

back. They're in good shape; go up and come back and see what it is that they see. I was disappointed, for example, in The Martian because I thought of all the things for a movie, and I think that they should remake it. What we need on Mars is a Black woman, and I was laughing yesterday; "We need a Black woman with some grits." Or maybe a yam. But we need a Black woman because to have a White man up there who's gonna grow potatoes is illogical.

RGS: See, that was my last word association: outer space.

NG: I'm a big fan and I think that it's so important that we get youngsters. We really have to get the inner city youngsters and, if I may, the Appalachian youngsters involved—the Appalachian Whites are involved. If you look at who were our first astronauts, they're all Appalachians, but we need to get our Black kids involved so that we can begin to envision space as where we are and how we create ourselves, and how we get along with—. So we know that we need Black women to be a part of space because they get along with and find a way to love everything, because we found a way to love people here in America.

RGS: And I ask you that because I've seen other places where you've called yourself a "Futurist." When you've talked about space and looking forward. So I wanted to ask you that. You also talked a lot about, in other interviews, your mother. You said that, "We get poetry through our mothers." Now what is a way that your mom or your grandmother or other female members have inspired the word?

NG: I think you pay attention to them. You see what they're doing. And I've been very lucky because I learned to cook with my grandmother, but I cook with mommy, and I made beans the other day because it's cold. And I just had this thing, I just wanted some northern beans and some jowl bacon, and it was so good. And I said to a friend, "But it wasn't my mother's beans." And I cannot make my mother's beans, because I don't smoke and I think that a part of what she did, she would—so there must have been something about smoking. There was something that she did, but I cooked with a lot of my friends, including Maya. And Maya and I used to love—because Maya thought she was, well, Maya was a good cook. I was gonna say she thought she was a good cook, but she was a good cook. But I thought I made better lamb. I made a rack of lamb. I thought my lamb was better and Maya thought hers was better, and we had this argument. And I used to cook with Edna Lewis, who was also a great chef, so, knowing those people and watching how they do things, you're watching poetry. And I mean, I enjoy it. I was just very lucky to know the people that I know and had a lot to do with my age and had a lot to do with the fact that when you meet people and you like them, you continue relationships.

RGS: Yes you do. I want to go back to what you said about sending Black women into space because I've seen other places where you said that you felt like that you are the "excellent representation."

NG: I would've been.

RGS: What makes Nikki Giovanni the "representative from Earth" to the extraterrestrials out there in the world?

NG: Well first of all, I don't want anything. And I think that's incredibly important because Earth and especially right now, you look at the fools that we have. You look at Donald Trump and the fools.

RGS: The fools.

NG: And they want things, but I don't want anything. I'm interested in people so. If I'm on Mars, I'm gonna find out who are you, and what do you do, and "Let's take some grits." "I have grits on Earth; well, do you?" I mean I think that I get along with people. The reason that I can't go into space, and I've said that to some high school students I was talking to recently, is that I grew up in a generation that smoked. We are the generation of segregation, but we also smoked and I had a lung cancer, and my left lung was removed. And I'm fortunate to be alive but I cannot—Dr. Bowland—I can't go into space. And I had lunch with him and he said "[inaudible at 13:28] we can send you into space, but we can't bring you back." And they can't bring me back because coming back into gravity, your organs move around, and if my stomach, for example, would move, or my liver would move, it would kill me. So I said, "Let's make a deal because I'm seventy-two years old. I'm not gonna live forever." People in my mother's family live probably into their nineties or so. I have—Agnes is ninety-four. I said "When I get into my late eighties, why don't you let me go into space?" Because I'm not gonna live much longer anyway, and when I die, you just open the hatch and just let me out. And then the kids can look on Earth and say "Oh there goes Nikki."

RGS: [Laughter] Nikki Giovanni!

NG: There goes Nikki.

Source: Nikki Giovanni, Interview by Randi Gil-Sadler, January 19, 2016, Interview AAHP 396, African American History Project, Samuel Proctor Oral History Program, Joel Buchanan Archive of African American History, George Smathers Libraries, University of Florida, Gainesville, FL.

CONTRIBUTORS

Madison W. Cates is assistant professor of history at Coastal Carolina University.

Anthony M. Donaldson Jr. is assistant professor of history at Sewanee: The University of the South.

Ashley D. Farmer is associate professor of African and African diaspora studies and history at the University of Texas–Austin. She is the author of *Remaking Black Power: How Black Women Transformed an Era* and coeditor of *New Perspectives on the Black Intellectual Tradition*.

D'Weston Haywood is associate professor of history at Hunter College, City University of New York. He is the author of *Let Us Make Men: The Twentieth-Century Black Press and a Manly Vision for Racial Advancement*.

Jasmin A. Young is assistant professor of ethnic studies at the University of California–Riverside. She is coeditor of the *Black Power Encyclopedia: From "Black is Beautiful" to Urban Uprisings* and author of "Gloria Richardson, Armed Self-Defense, and Black Liberation in Cambridge, Maryland," published in *The Journal of African American History*.

INDEX

Abiodun, Nehanda, 63
Abubakari, Dara (Virginia Collins), 56–57
Activism: and archival methods, 28; children, impact on, 68–69n33; community organizing, 23–24; and family histories, 56–57; oral history and security of activists, 63–64; and oral history collection, 58–59
African culture, stereotypes of, 51
African Liberation Day, 4
Afro-American Association (AAA), 58
Afrofuturism, 3, 11, 97, 101
Ageism, 2–3
Ahmad, Muhammad, 31
Alexander, Roberta, 58
Ali, Muhammad, 102
Allen, Ernie, 58
Amen-Allah, Kenyatto, 59
American Friends Service Committee (AFSC), 42
Archival material: access to, 30; Civil Rights Movement (CRM) vs. Black Power Movement (BPM), 2; definitions of, 27; primary sources, 9
Archival methodology, 12, 15n35; activism, impact of, 28; Black Power Studies vs. traditional, 3; digital resources, 10; diversity, need for, 28–29; ethical frameworks for, 36–39; metaphors for, 29–30, 34; and power dynamics, 29, 31–32; principle of provenance, 28; racism *vs.* inclusivity, 34–36; *respect des fonds*, 28
Atlanta, Georgia: Hunter Street, 47
Atlanta University Complex, 47
ATLiens (Outkast), 3

Attack of the Crab Monsters (film), 82
Authors' methodology, 7–8, 9–12; case studies, 9

Bakara, Amiri, 17
Baker, Ella, 5
Baker, General, 61
Baraka, Amiri, 31
Barnes, Elendar, 55
The Beast from 20,000 Fathoms (film), 82
Bennett, Lerone, Jr., 4
Berrey, Stephen, 57
Black Against Empire (Bloom & Martin), 4, 26
The Black Arts Movement (Smethurst), 26
Black Campus Movement, 48, 51
Black community: cultural impact of, 8, 51
Black Consciousness Movement, 19, 50–51
Black Futures (Drew & Wortham), 7
Black History: misinterpretations of, 5
Black Liberation: Elijah Muhammad, 11; freedom struggles, 53–54
Black Liberation Army (BLA), 5, 55, 63
Black Lives Matter, 7
Black media, 4
Black mysticism, 80
Black Nationalism, 79, 80, 88, 90
Black Panther (film series), 3
Black Panther Party (BPP), 1; antipoverty programs, 1; formation (1966), 19, 20–21; gender roles, 22; platform, 90; social programs, 55
The Black Panther Party, Reconsidered (Jones), 25
Black Power (Carmichael & Hamilton), 5

Index

Black Power Archives Oral History Project, 58
Black Power Beyond Borders (Slate), 26
Black Power Chronicles (SNCC), 58–59
Black Power Digital Archive (BPDA), 10
Black Power Movement (BPM), 1; and Black Panther Party formation, 19; contrasted with Civil Rights Movement, 53–54, 57, 65n3; goals of, 6; legacy and impact, 26; 1966 as turning point, 5; paradoxes of, 4–5; perceptions of, 33; resistance to, 50, 53; white critiques of, 4
Black Power Movement (BPM) archival material, 2; Black Power Digital Archive (BPDA), 10, 54, 62–65; dearth of, 26–27; dearth of, claims of, 32; "disorderly distribution," 9, 32–33; ethical frameworks for, 36–39; family histories, 56–57; first-person accounts in historiography, 25–26; future directions/new visions, 32–36; gaps in, 31; oral history, 54–57; oral history, need for, 10; oral history collections, 8–9, 57–60; and power dynamics, 27–28, 33–34; survey of, 27–32
Black Power Studies, 1–2, 26, 58; ageism, 2–3; primary sources, need for preservation, 2; social programs, 68–69n33
Black Studies, 51; as academic discipline, 1–2
Blain, Keisha, 26
Bland, Sandra, 7, 23
Blight, David, 6
Bloody Lowndes (Jeffries), 6
Bloom, Joshua, 4, 26
Bond, Julian, 1
Brown, Elaine, 25
Brown, H. Rap, 89
Brown, James, 4
Brundage, W. Fitzhugh, 15n35
Bukhari, Safiya, 55
Burnham, Dorothy Challenor, 56
Burnham, Linda, 56, 57
Burnham, Louis Everett, 56

Carmichael, Stokely, 1, 4, 5–6, 18, 49, 50, 89–90; SNCC leadership, 19–20
Case study methodology, 9
Cecelski, David, 11–12; Mabel Williams interview, 71–78

Cha-Jua, Sundiata Keita, 54, 65n3
Che-Lumumba Club, 58
Children: activism, impact on, 68–69n33; Black Panther Party community outreach, 55, 60
Civil Rights History Project Collection, 58
Civil Rights Movement (CRM), 1; archival material, 2; contrasted with Black Power Movement (BPM), 53–54, 57, 65n3
Clark, Mark, 64
Cleaver, Eldridge, 16, 17–18, 22–23
Cleaver, Kathleen, 2, 7, 11, 58; interview with, 16–24
Clinton, George, 3
Cobb, Charlie, 59
COINTELPRO, 5, 30, 36, 91–92
Cold War, 82–84
Combahee River Collective, 64
Community Alert Patrol, 58
Community organizing, 23–24
Concrete Demands (Williams), 26
Confederate States of America, 6
Congress of Racial Equality (CORE), 3, 89
Connolly, Brian, 32
Cox, Courtland, 59
Critical fabulation, 32
Crusader (NAACP newsletter), 60

Davis, Angela, 25
The Day the Earth Stood Still (film), 82
Delaney, Martin, 8
Democratic Party 1964 Convention, 49–50
Detroit uprising (1968), 5
Digital archives, 12; indexing tags, 64; Jasmin A. Young essay, 53–65
"The Dilemma of the American Negro Scholar" (Franklin), 35
Dixon, Aaron, 59
Dixon, Elmer, 59
Donaldson, Anthony M., Jr., 5
Douglass, Frederick, 8
Drake, Jarrett, 34
Drew, Kimberly, 7
Drew Ali, Noble, 80
Drum and Spear Bookstore and Press, 59
Du Bois, W.E.B., 8
Dunning, William, 6

Ebony (magazine), 4
Eisenhower, Dwight, 82
Evers, Medgar, 72
"Ezekiel's Wheel," 83, 91

Family histories, 101, 102, 104–5; of resistance, 56–57. *See also* Oral history
Fard, Wallace D., 80–81, 82, 83, 85
Farmer, Ashley D., 3, 5, 7, 8, 9–10; essay on Black Power archive, 25–39
Farrakhan, Louis, 86
FBI programs, 5; Nation of Islam (NOI) surveillance, 91–92; Reading Room, 30; surveillance of Nation of Islam, 81, 84–85, 87–88
"Fear of a Black Planet" (Public Enemy), 97
Featherstone, Ralph, 59
Feminist groups, 31. *See also* Gender roles
Fields, Barbara, 7
The Final Call (Nation of Islam newspaper), 4, 81
Fisk University, 16–17
Floyd, George, 7
Ford, Tanisha, 26
Forman, Jim, 17
Franklin, John Hope, 35
Freedom: definitions of, 53–54
Freedom Dreams (Kelley), 6
Freedom Now, 18
Freedom Summer Project (1964), 49
Fruit of Islam (FOI), 86
Fuentes, Marisa, 32
Fuller, Howard, 4
Fulton, Richard, 102

Garner, Eric, 23
Garvey, Marcus, 56, 80
Gender roles: in Black Panther Party, 22; Black women intellectuals, 33; family histories, 56–57; violence against women, 64; women-centered organizations, 31, 52; women in Black Panther Party, 55–56
Gerald 2X, 87
Gilroy, Paul, 80
Gil-Sadler, Randi: Nikki Giovanni interview, 101–5
Giovanni, Nikki, 7, 11; interview, 101–5

Gomez, Michael A., 86
Great Migration, 80
Guerrilla tactics, 5

Hamer, Fannie Lou, 49–50
Hamilton, Charles V., 5
Hampton, Fred, 64
Harding, Vincent, 65–66n4
Hart, Judy, 55
Hartman, Saidiya, 32
"The Hate that Hate Produced" (television documentary), 4, 84–85
Haywood, D'Weston, 4, 7, 8, 10–11, 97
Historically Black Colleges and Universities (HBCUs): archival records, 3
History, revisionist, concerning Confederacy, 6
Hogan, Wesley, 6
Hoover, J. Edgar, 30
House, Gloria, 61
Howard University, 57
Huggins, Erika, 58
Hurston, Zora Neale, 8

"I Have a Dream" speech (King), 6
Imperialism, resistance to, 4–5
Integration: Carmichael's 1966 speech, 5–6; NAACP efforts, 60

Jacobs, Harriet, 8
Jazz, 103
Jefferson, Thomas, 76
Jeffries, Hasan Kwame, 6
Jet (magazine), 4
Jim Crow policies, 6
Jimerson, Randall C., 29, 34
Johnson, Ethel Azalea, 60
Johnson, James Weldon, 8
Johnson, Raymond, 1
Jones, Charles, 25
Jones, LeRoi, 17, 31
Joseph, Peniel, 1–2, 7, 25–26, 53

Karenga, Ron, 89
Kelley, Robin D. G., 6, 80, 90
Kendi, Ibram X., 48
King, Martin Luther, Jr., 1, 72; "I Have a Dream" speech, 6

Knight, Michael Muhammad, 85
Ku Klux Klan (KKK), 60

Ladner, Dorie, 59
Lang, Clarence, 54, 65n3
Lawson, Jennifer, 59
Let Us Make Men (Haywood), 4
Lewis, Edna, 105
Lewis, Joan Tarika (Matilaba), 22, 55
Lewis, John, 19–20, 49
Liberated Threads (Ford), 26
Liiteracy, 26, 74
Long Movement thesis, 65n3
Lowndes County Black Panther Party, 37–38
Lowndes County Freedom Organization, 19

Majied, Eugene, 87
Malcolm X, 1, 85
Mallory, Mae, 36
Man: Whence, How and Whither (Besant), 85
Mapping projects, 64
March Against Fear (Meredith), 50
Marshall, Kerry James, 8
Martin, Trayvon, 23
Martin, Waldo, 4, 26
Matilaba (Joan Tarika Lewis), 22, 55
McCray, Ida, 55
McKissick, Floyd, 3, 4, 89
Meredith, James, 50
Meredith March, 18
Message to the Blackman (Muhammad), 88
Miami uprising (1980), 5
Middle Passage, 103
Mississippi Freedom Democratic Party, 49
Moore, Audley, 36
"Mother Plane," Nation of Islam, 83–84, 89, 91
MOVE (communal organization), 5
Mtume, Norma, 58
Muhammad, Elijah, 7, 11, 79; Black planet, 86–87, 89; *Message to the Blackman*, 88; *Muhammad Speaks* address (1962), 85–89, 97–100; Space Age, impact of, 82–84; *The Supreme Wisdom*, 83–84, 85
Muhammad Speaks (newspaper), 4, 11, 79–80, 85–89; Elijah Muhammad's address (1962), 85–89, 97–100

Mulford Act (1967), 21
Museums, dearth of Black Power, 3
Mutually Assured Destruction (MAD), 84
Myers, Josh, 2

Naeem, Abdul Basit, 91
National Aeronautics and Space Administration (NASA), 82, 103–104
National Association for the Advancement of Colored People (NAACP), 60
National Black Political Convention 1972 (Gary, Indiana), 64
National Council of Negro Women, 42, 51, 52
National Museum of African American History and Culture, 58
Nation of Islam (NOI), 4, 42; Black planet, 86–87, 89; Carmichael in *Muhammad Speaks*, 89–90; creation of, 80; Elijah Muhammad's leadership, 79–80; FBI surveillance, 81, 84–85, 87–88, 91–92; Fruit of Islam (FOI), 86; long-term goals, 90; "Mother Plane," 83–84, 89, 91; *Muhammad Speaks*, 85–89; platform, 90; *The Supreme Wisdom* (Muhammad), 83–84, 85
A Nation within a Nation (Woodard), 25
Newark uprising (1967), 5
Newton, Huey P., 1, 20, 22, 90; archival collection, 29
Nixon, Richard, 4
Nuclear Age, 83–84

Oral history: with aging activists, 63; Civil Rights Movement, 54; family histories, 56–57; Gwendolyn Zoharah Simmons interview, 42–52; impact of, 54–55; Kathleen Cleaver interview, 16–24; Mabel Williams interview, 71–78; and security of activists, 63–64. *See also* Family histories
Ortiz, Paul, 4
Outkast (hip hop duo), 3

Parliament-Funkadelic (band), 3
Patton, Gwen, 31, 37–38
Poetry, 101–2

Police brutality, 23–24
Poole, Elijah, 80–81. See also Muhammad, Elijah
Poverty: Black Panther Party (BPP) programs, 1, 55
Project Woman Power, 52
Provenance, principle of, 28
Provisional Government of the Republic of New Africa (PGRNA), 56, 63
Public Enemy (hip hop group), 97

Ra, Sun, 3
Racial pride, 3–4
Racial uprisings, 5
Racism, 44, 75. See also White supremacy
Radio Free Dixie (Tyson), 25
Ralph Bunche Oral History Collection, 57
Reconstruction, 6, 13n18
Remaking Black Power (Farmer), 26
Republic of New Africa (RNA), 30
Respect des fonds, 28
Revolutionary Action Movement (RAM), 5
The Revolution Has Come (Spencer), 26
Rice, Tamir, 23–24
Richardson, Judy, 59
Rickford, Russell, 26
Robinson, Cedric, 8
Ross, Lorretta, 56

San Francisco 8 case, 63–64, 70n44
"Say Her Name" campaign, 7
Science fiction films, 82
Seale, Robert "Bobby," 1, 21; imprisonment, 22–23
Seattle Civil Rights and Labor History Project, 59
Self-defense, Black Panther emphasis on, 1
Set the World on Fire (Blain), 26
Shakur, Assata, 55, 64
Simmons, Gwendolyn Zoharah, 7, 11; interview with, 42–52
Simmons, Michael, 51, 52
Slate, Nico, 26
Slave Narratives, WPA Project, 9
Smethurst, James, 26
Soulbook (journal), 58
Soul City project, 4

Southern Christian Leadership Conference (SCLC), 5–6
Southern Historical Collection (SHC) (UNC), 3
Space Age/Space Race, 81–82, 87, 103–104
Space is the Place (Sun Ra), 3
Spelman College, 42, 46–47, 48–49
Spencer, Robyn, 10, 26, 55
Stanford, Max, 31
Student Nonviolent Coordinating Committee (SNCC), 1, 89; Atlanta as base, 19; Black Power Chronicles (BPC), 58–59; campus programs, 17; Fisk University conference (1967), 16–17; Gwendolyn Z. Simmons' experience, 48–49; Legacy Project, 58, 68n26; Lowndes County Freedom Organization, 19
The Supreme Wisdom (Muhammad), 83–84

Taylor, Breonna, 7
Temple University, 52
Them! (film), 82
Theoharis, Jeanne, 53
Third World Women's Alliance (TWWA), 31, 56, 67n15
Tom and Ethel Bradley Center, 58
Trenholm State Community College, 31
Trouillot, Michel-Rolph, 31
Trump, Donald, 105
Tyson, Timothy, 25

University of North Carolina, Wilson Library, 3

Venia, Emma Lou, 102
Vietnam War, 51
Violence: Black Power activism and public perceptions, 5; Black self-defense, 61; against women, 64
Von Eschen, Penny, 11
Voter registration, 49

Waiting 'Til the Midnight Hour (Joseph), 25–26
Walker, David, 8
Walker, Margaret, 17
Wallace, Mike, 4, 84
Washington, Booker T., 8
Washington, George, 76

Watson, Agnes Margery, 102
Watson, Anne-Elizabeth, 102
Watson, Cornelia, 102
Watson, Emma Lou, 102
Watson, John Brown, 102
Watson, Yolande Cornelia, 102
Wattstax concert, 64
Watts uprising (1965), 5
Weapons and Mulford Act (1967), 21
We Are an African People (Rickford), 26
Wheatley, Phillis, 8
"Wheel of Ezekiel," 83, 91
White supremacy, 1, 6, 71, 84, 92. *See also* Racism
William, Robert F., 25
William Dunning School, 6
Williams, John, 61

Williams, Mabel, 7, 10, 11–12, 60–62; interview with, 71–78
Williams, Rhonda, 10, 26, 55–56
Williams, Robert F., 31, 60; in Mabel Williams' interview, 71–78
Williams, Shamseddin, 59
Women-centered organizations, 31, 52. *See also* Gender roles
Woodard, Komozi, 25
World War II, 81
Wortham, Jenna, 7
WPA (Works Progress Administration) Project Slave Narratives, 9

Young, Jasmin A., 7, 8–9, 10; essay on oral history digital archive, 53–65
Young Communist League, 56

Frontiers of the American South
Edited by William A. Link

United States Reconstruction across the Americas, edited by William A. Link (2019)
Reckoning with Rebellion: War and Sovereignty in the Nineteenth Century, by Aaron Sheehan-Dean (2020)
Sisterly Networks: Fifty Years of Southern Women's Histories, edited by Catherine Clinton (2020)
Futures of Black Power: Reimagining the Black Past, edited by Anthony M. Donaldson Jr. and Madison W. Cates (2025)

www.ingramcontent.com/pod-product-compliance
Lightning Source LLC
Chambersburg PA
CBHW030444231225
37194CB00022B/435